Desegregation and Hispanic Students: A Community Perspective

Tony Baéz
Ricardo R. Fernández
Judith T. Guskin

NATIONAL CLEARINGHOUSE
FOR BILINGUAL EDUCATION

This document is published by InterAmerica Research Associates, Inc., pursuant to contract NIE 400-77-0101 to operate the National Clearinghouse for Bilingual Education. The National Clearinghouse for Bilingual Education is jointly funded by the National Institute of Education and the Office of Bilingual Education and Minority Languages Affairs, U.S. Department of Education. Contractors undertaking such projects under government sponsorship are encouraged to express their judgment freely in professional and technical matters; the views expressed in this publication do not necessarily reflect the views of the sponsoring agencies.

InterAmerica Research Associates, Inc. d/b/a
National Clearinghouse for Bilingual Education
1300 Wilson Boulevard, Suite B2-11
Rosslyn, Virginia 22209
(703) 522-0710/(800) 336-4560

Cover design by J. Nick Davis, Sans Serif Graphics, Arlington, Virginia
Typesetting by Eagle One Graphics, Inc., Lanham, Maryland

Library of Congress Catalog Card Number: 80-80311
ISBN: 0-89763-023-8
First printing 1980
Printed in USA

10   9   8   7   6   5   4   3   2

Contents

Foreword

The National Clearinghouse for Bilingual Education is pleased to present this very thorough examination of the interaction of desegregation and bilingual education in Milwaukee, Wisconsin. It is our hope that this publication will serve other communities which are involved in blending desegregation and bilingual education into effective educational programs for children. The authors present a lively, step-by-step description of grass roots community participation, with various individuals, factions, and points of view. The original version of this paper was part of a series on desegregation and bilingual education developed under the sponsorship of the National Institute of Education in 1978; the authors have updated and expanded that original document.

Luis Antonio (Tony) Baéz was born and reared in Puerto Rico. In 1970 he moved to Chicago, coming to Milwaukee in 1971 to study and work in community organizations. He received a B.A. in education from the University of Wisconsin—Milwaukee in 1973 and served as parent coordinator for the City-Wide Bilingual Bicultural Advisory Committee from 1975-1977. From 1977-1979, Mr. Baéz was program coordinator at the Midwest National Origin Desegregation Assistance Center, where he was involved in the design of Title VI Lau compliance plans for school districts throughout the Midwest. He is a speaker and consultant on parent involvement, bilingual education, and school desegregation and has authored articles and other materials in these areas.

Ricardo R. Fernández is the director of the Midwest National Origin Desegregation Assistance Center, the 1980-81 president of the National Association for Bilingual Education, and an associate professor in the Department of Cultural Foundations of Education at the University of Wisconsin—Milwaukee. Dr. Fernández has been active in foreign language education and bilingual education for more than a decade. He has taught at several institutions (Marquette University, Princeton University, Inter-American University of Puerto Rico, University of Guam) and has published widely on the topics of bilingual education and school desegregation. Dr. Fernández has served on the board of the Curriculum Adaptation Network for Bilingual Bicultural Education (Project CANBBE), the board of the National Puerto Rican Task Force on Education Policy, and the advisory committee to the National Review Panel on School Desegregation Research. He has been a consultant to various agencies, including the U.S. Office of Education, the National Institute of Education, the Illinois Office of Education, and the National Education Task Force de la Raza. He holds a Ph.D. in romance languages from Princeton University.

Judith T. Guskin is a senior program associate with the Midwest National Origin Desegregation Assistance Center in Milwaukee, Wisconsin, and an adjunct associate professor of anthropology at the University of Wisconsin—Parkside. She formerly was a consultant with the Midwest Resource Center, a Title VII Bilingual Education Training Resource Center located in Illinois. Dr. Guskin served as assistant professor at Clark University in Massachusetts where she taught courses on bilingualism. She was an ESL teacher trainer in Thailand and has had administrative responsibilities related to migrant education, VISTA, and the Peace Corps. While at the University of Michigan, Dr. Guskin conducted research on teacher attitudes toward linguistic variation and on the effects of high school racial climates on students and teachers. Among her publications are a chapter on first and second language acquisition in *The Bilingual Child* (Academic Press, 1976, edited by A. Simoes) and an article on desegregation and bilingual education (with Ricardo Fernández in *Bilingual Education*, Avery Publishing Group, 1978, edited by H. LaFontaine, B. Persky, and L. Golubchick). Dr. Guskin received her Ph.D. from the University of Michigan.

One of the functions of the National Clearinghouse for Bilingual Education is to publish documents addressing the specific informational needs of the bilingual education field. We are pleased to add this publication to our growing list of titles. Subsequent Clearinghouse products will similarly seek to contribute to information and knowledge which can assist in the education of minority culture and language groups in the United States.

National Clearinghouse for Bilingual Education

Desegregation and Hispanic Students:
A Community Perspective

Introduction

This is a case study of the desegregation process in Milwaukee's Public Schools and the participation of the Hispanic community in that process through the efforts of a parent-community group—the City-Wide Bilingual Bicultural Advisory Committee (CWBBAC)—to safeguard the rights of Hispanic students to equal educational opportunity. It is an attempt to delineate with some specificity the legal and political decision-making process involved when a major city prepares and implements a school desegregation plan, a plan which emerged as a direct result of the Board of School Directors having been found guilty of intentionally operating a segregated school system in violation of the United States' Constitution (*Armstrong* v. *O'Connell*, C.A. No. 65-C-173, Eastern District of Wisconsin, January 19, 1976).[1]

The issues and principal actors usually found in a school desegregation situation are all present: the judge and the court-appointed Special Master; the School Board, with its various factions; the school administrators who develop a plan; the teachers' union, which intervenes to protect the interests of its members; the media (radio, TV, and newspapers), which report on developments as they occur; the various groups and organizations throughout the community promoting their particular interests. This case enables us to examine in some detail how a community has dealt and continues to deal with issues affecting cities with multiethnic populations. Its particular focus is on the demands made by Hispanics for their educational needs and legal rights within the context of court-ordered desegregation. Of special interest are the issues related to the legal definitions used by courts and desegregation planners and their potential negative impact on Hispanics. Two are crucial: (1) Are Hispanics an identifiable ethnic/racial group or are they to be categorized as "White" or "non-Black" in the planning process?; (2) How will ratios imposed by court order apply to Hispanic students and bilingual teachers?

It would be inappropriate to begin a discussion of the case and its aftermath in a vacuum; therefore, some historical background is necessary about the growth of Milwaukee over the past twenty-five years and how some federal, state, and local policies have affected its development. These conditions have created the environment where the drama of desegregation is played out. It is also necessary to know something about the city's history and its ethnic, social, economic, and political dimensions. State policies promulgated in the 1970s, such as equalization of taxes between rich and poor school districts, voluntary transfers for desegregation and integration, and mandatory bilingual bicultural education, have had an obvious impact on the city and need to be reviewed.

In our conclusions we point out some of the key variables involved in determining the outcome of school desegregation planning and implementation as it has affected Hispanics in this midwestern city. While it is impossible to capture fully the dynamism and complexity of the process and the changing roles and scenarios which developed over time, we have highlighted the political context of decision making involved in developing a desegregation plan, from the perspective of Hispanics. The interaction between Hispanics and Blacks and the resulting compromises are also presented. The process of school desegregation which emerges from this account can be characterized as essentially a political solution framed within the limits of a judicial decree which allows the implementation to be worked out in the public arena of competing group and community interests.

Historical and Comparative Perspective

The issues of implementing both desegregation and bilingual education in the cities outside the South in the 1970s are not only legal ones, though the courts are the arena in which Blacks and Hispanics must interact with each other and with Whites to negotiate political settlements related to educational policy since minorities have little influence concerning schools and urban development. Nor are the issues only pedagogical. Both minority groups need additional services to remedy past discrimination, to modify school practices to take into account ethnic differences and respect ethnic pride, to focus attention on their needs as schools expand educational options (such as magnet schools) as part of desegregation, and to institute more affirmative hiring. It is obvious that the questions "Who benefits most from changes?" and "Who bears most of the burden?" cause conflict and require compromise. Since initial steps were taken toward desegregation outside the South, Hispanic educational concerns have gained national recognition and, therefore, are being considered by some courts and some school administrations in designing appropriate remedies for today's multiethnic school systems. The imperative for including these concerns is clear, even if the implementation strategies are not.

Underlying the current legal battles for equal educational opportunity is the national dilemma regarding the future of our cities which poses serious financial, political, racial, and educational problems. Desegregation issues hold up a mirror to our cities in which we can see the interconnection of segregation and discrimination with decisions to expand freeways, build industrial parks in the suburbs, tear down housing without replacement for those displaced, build new schools in suburbs and add on to crowded, old ones in the inner cores of the cities. Basic values producing decisions leading to laissez-faire industrial growth and discrimination against minority groups have been creating the current realities for many years.

The story of the current crisis over desegregation in Milwaukee today cannot be understood by viewing a few frames presenting current events, for they are part of a moving picture of social change. Like all social change,

3

the Milwaukee situation is produced by policies, intergroup relationships, and historical circumstances as well as the individual actions of a few people interested in and capable of bringing about modification in the flow of events. Changes in Milwaukee, a school system with 91,943 pupils, including 45 percent (41,530) Blacks and 6 percent (5,175) Hispanics (as of Sept. 1977), and a $294 million budget, can highlight problems faced by other cities with similar characteristics, for the growth of urban schooling in the U.S. has followed similar patterns. While the current court case and recent actors are in the foreground, the attitudes and events involved in the story of desegregation and bilingual education in Milwaukee today reflect developments over several decades.

Early History: First World War Period

The neighborhood school policy so vigorously defended by the School Board during the court case on desegregation began in 1919. What was Milwaukee like at that time? At the onset of the First World War almost a third of the nation's total population was foreign born. The first wave to arrive in Milwaukee, a large group of Germans, was followed by a highly diversified migration from eastern and southern Europe, and others. Due to this early immigration, one of five citizens of Milwaukee today is a child of foreign-born parents.[2]

Around the First World War, politicians and business leaders worried about linguistic and cultural diversity but continued to benefit from the skills and labor of immigrant workers. In Milwaukee, as in other cities, there was at first a permissive attitude toward the foreign-language press and use of the native language in school when local desire warranted.[3] German and Polish were taught in private and public schools in Milwaukee. However, a national outbreak of fear and repression lead to the National Origins Act, national immigration legislation passed in 1924, which set rigid quotas on immigration from southern and eastern Europe and Asia. The non-English press was under attack, as were the languages of those providing the labor force to build the industrial might of America. In the name of patriotism, militant Americanization-movement members tried to produce rapid homogenization. Fifteen state legislatures, including Wisconsin's, passed laws mandating that only English be taught in the schools.[4] At first the Germans and Poles of Milwaukee resisted these efforts, but soon ethnic pride was traded for the tangible benefits linked with acceptability and political power.

Second-generation attitudes of shame, rejection, and ambivalence toward language and culture were shaped by policies toward immigrants. Today in Milwaukee many German Americans recall the intense pressures placed on their fathers to change their names and to stop speaking German in public in order to get employment. They grew up knowing that the German-language newspapers had been forced to close down and that, despite the desires of many parents, teaching German in elementary schools had been stopped.

However, interest in ethnic diversity and public support for culture did not disappear as a consequence of the environment created by World War I. Even today, under the desegregation plan, when a second-language proficiency, elementary magnet school was proposed that would allow children to learn subject matter in a bilingual English-German program, the German-American Association indicated support. Although initial interest on the part of White parents was low, after aggressive recruitment by administrators, the school recruited enough pupils, including Black students, to open in September 1977. Also, as in many other cities, each year Milwaukeeans celebrate the diversity of their community during a Folk Fair. Ethnic politics, ethnic neighborhoods and organizations exist side by side with the denial of ethnic importance in American life. The traditional American ambivalence toward ethnicity continues. As Andrew Greeley has said, we praise the melting pot out of one side of our mouth and honor cultural pluralism out of the other.[5]

In the period between wars, Milwaukee grew and developed into a major city, even though it was overshadowed by the prominence of Chicago. Industrialization continued to foster a multiethnic city. Like Chicago and Detroit, the magnet of job possibilities, coupled with helping networks of family and friends, made Milwaukee prosper, and it became the industrial center for the state. Immigration continued into the 1930s. At that time in neighboring Racine, nearly 60 percent of the city was foreign born.[6] In 1939 Milwaukee became the seventh largest Polish center in America with 120,000 Poles. Milwaukee was successful not because it eliminated diversity, but because it created the possibility for more of it.

World War II to the Present:
Rapid Growth and Racial Segregation

World War II led to a change in the racial and ethnic makeup of the migrants to the city of Milwaukee. Blacks, leaving the South in search of jobs, settled in the Midwest where they found factory work. The rise in the city's Black population between 1950 and 1970 was in excess of 500 percent. While the Black population at least doubled in Chicago, and Detroit as well, Milwaukee's sustained rate of growth was the highest of any large city in the country. The Mexican and Puerto Rican population in the city also started to grow.

The total land area of the city nearly doubled, largely due to aggressive annexation policies, from forty-nine to ninety-two square miles. Suburban growth continued, leaving a ring of eighteen suburbs around the city. This growth was aided by 150 miles of new freeways leading increasing numbers of White Milwaukeeans out of the city limits in search of the American ideal—a home, a lawn mower, and a neighborhood of people similar to themselves. Blacks and Hispanics inherited the older homes in the inner core, and the older schools. The Black and Hispanic population was younger, and the school population in the inner city reflected this fact.

While the need grew for new schools in the outlying areas to serve the

Whites moving there, the same need arose in the inner city as well. The School Board ignored the obviously increasing segregation and continued to renovate older schools for Black children and build new ones for Whites.[7] Between 1950 and 1960 the number of elementary schools increased from 79 to 115, and the number of junior highs from 4 to 12. Between 1950-51 and 1973-74, the total number of schools increased by 71 percent, making Milwaukee the eleventh largest school system in the country as well as one of the most segregated.

Urban growth was not only reflected in the changing ethnic and racial composition of neighborhoods and schools, but also in changes in the tax base. School costs increased with a concomitant rise in school levies (100 percent in the years 1960-1970), and the tax structure became more unfair, as citizens in the suburbs continued to use city services, such as water, sewage, and cultural activities, and also received a larger share of state taxes returned to their suburban neighborhoods. For example, in 1965 suburban municipalities received about 53 percent of revenues from state-shared taxes, while the city received only 24 percent.

There were some local and federal efforts to develop reforms, but many ended in frustration and failure, or had the effect of increasing racial and class segregation rather than moderating it. Elected officials, especially the mayor, tried to develop metropolitan solutions to urban social and resource problems. The hope was to trade jobs, transportation, water and sewage services for a fairer share of tax monies to help rebuild old housing, provide care for the elderly, and educate the children of the poor.[8] A commission of economic and civic leaders was set up in the 1950s, but their efforts failed.[9] Federal dollars were made available, but the combined effects of Federal Housing Administration policies, mortgage programs for veterans, and their implementation by local bankers, real estate agents, and builders led to increased segregation.

By 1970 the residential segregation process was nearly complete. Almost 90 percent of the nearly 105,000 Blacks lived in an area which was 65-75 percent Black. The Hispanic population was more dispersed, but both groups shared the poorest housing and oldest schools. Thus, while the *Brown* decision in 1954 outlawed segregation in schools, in the decades that followed, cities outside the South experienced a rapid growth in minority populations and a concomitant development of residential and school segregation. Actions and failures to act on the part of local and federal officials helped produce the social conditions that became inflamed in the 1960s. Milwaukee was no exception to these patterns.

The Turbulent Sixties:
Black Demands and White Resistance

The 1960s in Milwaukee were ushered in by clashes between police and young Blacks. These had become frequent enough to cause the mayor in 1959 to set up the Study Committee on Social Problems in the Inner Core Area of the city. The present mayor took office in April of 1960 and found little guidance in the way of specific recommendations as a result of the study. He decided to organize a commission to implement some solutions to general social problems, not just racial issues. The commission, later called the Social Development Commission (SDC), became the structure to implement the programs paid for by $5 million of federal antipoverty money awarded to Milwaukee in 1964. The SDC shared similar characteristics to other War on Poverty programs. Internal strife which existed between the representatives of the poor and the officials on the board ended with most of the control remaining in the mayor's hands. Later, the SDC was to evolve independently of the mayor's office into a larger and heavily funded structure.

Blacks did not have much power in Milwaukee. In 1968, they held only 6 of 121 elected positions in the county and 1 of 81 policy-making posts in city government. In the schools, only 5 of 157 principals were Black.[10] In 1963 a Black state assemblyman from Milwaukee, who was also president of the state NAACP, pressured the elected State Superintendent of Public Instruction to end segregation in Milwaukee. Similar actions were being taken by Blacks in other parts of the country. Since the local decision-making structures were not representative, attention to the needs of Blacks was sought through actions that would attract media coverage. While the courts were still focusing on a resistant South, northern and eastern cities faced demands and boycotts for desegregation. In ninety-one cities, 61 percent of the first demands for desegregated schooling were made between 1963 and 1965.[11] Similar to what happened in Milwaukee, the first demand was usually initiated by the NAACP and was generally a diffuse call for the school system to do something about segregation.

The response of most school boards was resistance. In the ninety-one cities studied by Kirby et al.,[12] one-fourth did nothing at all while 51 percent made some symbolic gesture, but took no immediate remedial action which affected students attending school. Milwaukee's School Board responded by appointing a committee. However, the recommendations of the committee were all rejected. This incident set the tone for a pattern of resistance that continues to the present time. Again, this was not unique to Milwaukee. As a study of desegregation in northern cities of the time indicated, the initial response usually set the tone for future school board actions.[13]

Frustration and anger led Blacks to organize boycotts and demonstrations. The marches and sit-ins of the sixties produced community organizations capable of providing leadership in the battle for desegregation. In Milwaukee, a new organization called the Milwaukee United School Integration Committee (MUSIC) was formed; it planned several school boycotts and demonstrations that produced media coverage.[14] Finally, in 1965, a formal desegregation suit was filed in federal court.[15]

The issue of open housing, one which involved mostly Blacks under the general leadership of an activist Catholic priest, James Groppi, had a major effect on Milwaukeeans because of embarrassment created by national media coverage. However, there was little change. Just as the School Board resisted the school boycotts and demands for desegregation, Mayor Henry

Maier and the Common Council resisted Father Groppi and his youthful protesters. The issue did not go away, even though the Common Council from 1962-1967 consistently turned down proposed open housing legislation eighteen to one, the only dissenter being a Black member of the council.

Frustration reached a peak in 1967. By that year little progress was being made in terms of eliminating discrimination or segregation. Although more money was spent on studies,[16] the Common Council refused to submit a proposal for a Model Cities program.[17] That same year the U.S. Commission on Civil Rights indicated in its report *Racial Isolation in the Schools* that Milwaukee ranked the lowest of seven cities examined for failure to have any policy to remedy segregation in schools.[18]

1967 was the year of the riots. If youths could not bring about changes by demands, boycotts, and protests, they would burn down the city. Flames and rocks replaced singing marchers in Milwaukee and elsewhere in the nation. Maier called in the National Guard, and citizens cried out in dismay and disbelief that this kind of urban chaos could be happening in Milwaukee, that city of Old World charm and easygoing good nature, good living, and geniality typified by the German word *Gemütlichkeit*. A local survey indicated that most rioters were unemployed local youth and gave as cause of the riots the social ills that were being ignored, but most White Milwaukeeans perceived the problem as caused by outsiders and the remedy as more police.[19]

Milwaukee's representatives of the established and powerful institutions—the business leaders, the mayor and the Common Council, the School Board, labor leaders—maintained a posture of noninvolvement. Maier maintained his dominant political position by refusing to meet with demonstrators, avoiding taking stands on issues like desegregation, and stressing his inability to solve city problems that required metropolitan solutions. His behavior was thus similar to most mayors who try not to act on controversial issues unless the conflict escalates.[20] Since he inherited a weak mayoral form of city government, Maier had to manage to keep in tune with the Common Council, and the fact that he has been mayor since 1960 attests to his skill in doing so. Elected officials continue to dominate the city's power structure.[21] The business leaders were not a cohesive group and, while supporting the cultural development of the city, did not wish to become active in influencing changes related to race relations that would not have the support of most Milwaukeeans.

When civic leadership is inactive and elected officials do not take public and positive stands, school desegregation conflicts continue and often escalate in the context of official resistance, as well as official silence. The forces against desegregation grow stronger. Conflict brings the issue to the attention of the public; but without support and resources for resolution (for example, the lack of public supportive stands by elected officials), it continues to polarize groups and create more fragmentation. Ultimately the issue is left to community groups, the media, the courts, and the school boards.

8

Until 1979 the School Board in Milwaukee was a fifteen-member independent unit elected at large for staggered six-year terms. Traditionally it had not represented the interests of minority and poor students. Recent state legislation has changed the number of members and the process by which they are elected, but the political inclination of its membership continues to vary with each election. Until 1979 the power had been in the hands of what Milwaukeeans called the "conservative" majority, although the board's "liberal" faction had been very vocal in their defense of both community involvement and desegregation. Thus, the board's actions have to be understood in this context.[22]

During the 1960s the board's reaction to charges of segregation was to deny official wrongdoing and to resist efforts by local groups to desegregate while funding compensatory education programs. In so doing it was not acting differently than most school boards in large cities. In the ninety-one cities studied by Kirby et al., 79 percent eventually initiated compensatory education and, like Milwaukee, most did so within the first few months of demands for desegregation.[23] Open enrollment policies were also common in those cities and occurred in Milwaukee as well. The result was increased segregation as Whites moved to schools where they were in large numbers. Since the initial charges of segregation, the board has defended its neighborhood school policy. Millions of dollars were spent on busing although almost none of it was spent to support desegregation. On the contrary, White students were bused to White schools and Black students, sometimes in intact segregated classes, to Black and White schools.

Hispanics Focus Efforts on Education in the Sixties and Seventies

The Hispanic community in Milwaukee had grown in the fifties and sixties just as the Black community had grown. The first significant numbers of Mexicans came to Milwaukee in the early 1920s, recruited as strike breakers by local tanneries. After World War II the first Puerto Ricans began arriving, recruited directly from Puerto Rico by local industry or moving from Chicago and other midwestern cities. By 1970 the U.S. Census reported almost 23,000 Spanish-speaking persons in Milwaukee. Given the median age of Hispanics (under twenty) and a high birth rate, the community grew in the seventies. Current estimates place their numbers at around 35,000.

Although there has always existed a wealth of activity among Hispanics in Milwaukee, the major organizations developed around social and cultural endeavors, with minimal energies devoted to other areas. By the midsixties, in part as a natural outgrowth of the times and the issues being debated, the first attempts at organizing among Hispanics for political and socioeconomic gains were seen, and education proved to be a very fertile area for community organizers to rally around and formulate demands.

Nationwide, during the sixties, Hispanics began to focus more of their protests and political organizing efforts on school reform. In addition to the programs for Cuban refugees in the sixties in Florida, Hispanics in many other areas of the country demanded new programs to meet the needs of their children. These demands resulted in the passage of the federal Bilingual Education Act (Title VII, Elementary and Secondary Education Act) in 1968 which provided some financial incentives for school districts to develop demonstration projects in bilingual education.

When the Bilingual Education Act was passed by Congress, Milwaukee was ready to move into a new educational arena. In terms of educational services, Milwaukee Public Schools had responded to the influx of Puerto Ricans and Mexicans in the fifties by expanding its English-as-a-second-language (ESL) programs. Given this new federal incentive, an application for funds to operate a pilot bilingual education program in one school was submitted to the U.S. Office of Education. A grant was received in the spring of 1969, and a small program was started in the fall at Vieau Elementary, a predominantly Hispanic school located on the near south side of the city. This successful initial program added a classroom every year in order to provide continuity for students enrolled the previous year. Other schools were added in the early seventies.[24]

A bilingual (Spanish-English) materials development center was established in Milwaukee in 1971 as part of a national project, the Curriculum Adaptation Network for Bilingual Bicultural Education (CANBBE). Although this project's scope of work was regional, the district's bilingual education program benefited from the center's materials production and attendant resources; furthermore, the project helped confirm Milwaukee's national reputation as a center for quality bilingual programming in public schools.

The year 1970 was a year of growing organization and militancy on the part of the local Hispanic community. In 1970 the Council for the Education of Latin Americans (CELA) demanded that an academic services program be established for Hispanic students at the University of Wisconsin–Milwaukee. This effort was successful. Later, claims of police brutality brought about clashes between Hispanic marchers and police in 1971. This led the governor of Wisconsin to establish a task force to study the problems facing the Spanish-speaking in Wisconsin, giving state recognition to the needs of the Hispanic community.

By 1972 the community's attention began to shift toward the public schools, and in the spring of 1973 Chicano and Puerto Rican organizers collaborated to form a committee which would address the needs of Hispanic students in the city's public schools. In 1974 the City-Wide Bilingual Bicultural Advisory Committee (CWBBAC) was recognized by the Milwaukee Board of School Directors as "the official advisory board for bilingual bicultural education within Milwaukee Public Schools on all matters related to Hispanics, to review on a continual basis bilingual bicultural programs, and to recommend improvements or expansions, and participate in interviewing and recommending for hiring bilingual/bicultural personnel."[25] Later, this committee was to play a key role in promoting the rights of Hispanic students during the desegregation process.

In May of that year, after long and protracted negotiations between the CWBBAC and the Milwaukee school administration, a series of recommendations were forwarded to the School Board, which approved them unanimously. Among the most important of these was a motion supporting the concept and implementation of a developmental (maintenance) bilingual bicultural education program in Spanish and, if needed and wanted by parents, in other languages as well. This new thrust away from a strictly transitional approach to another, whose purpose was to develop functional, coordinate bilinguality in students, constituted a milestone for Milwaukee public schools. In addition, the district enabled the program to continue and expand by adding local funds in anticipation of an eventual reduction in the level of federal financial support. With the constant support of the CWBBAC, the Milwaukee bilingual program continued to grow in numbers of students and staff.

Meanwhile, nationally, the seventies brought significant legal actions which defined equal educational opportunity for Hispanics. The first such action was the issuance by the Department of Health, Education, and Welfare (HEW) of its now-renowned May 25, 1970 memorandum, which states in part:

> Where inability to speak and understand the English language excludes national origin-minority group children from effective participation in the educational program offered by a school district, the district must take affirmative steps to rectify the language deficiency in order to open its instructional program to these students.

The content of this memorandum, and HEW's authority to formulate such guidelines, were later upheld by the U.S. Supreme Court in *Lau* v. *Nichols*.[26] This memorandum was sent to all chief state school officers and to over 300 districts throughout the country with 5 percent or more national origin minority group children enrolled in their schools. Recognition was given to unique educational needs based on language used by children, and the schools' refusal to address these needs became obvious and no longer acceptable to the Office for Civil Rights (HEW).

As a result of a series of suits by Mexican American parents in the Southwest, the courts started to define the rights of Hispanic students in public schools for purposes of equal protection and to fashion remedies that would correct violations of those rights. Thus, in *Cisneros* v. *Corpus Christi*[27] much attention was given to considering Hispanics as an identifiable ethnic minority group for purposes of desegregation and to designing a remedy that would include programs aimed at meeting their educational needs, namely bilingual education. In *U.S.* v. *Texas* (San Felipe-Del Rio),[28] the court went further by ordering a comprehensive bilingual instructional program for Mexican children. This was also the case in *Serna* v. *Portales*[29] where a later finding of violation was made under Title VI, Section 601 of the Civil Rights Act of 1964, in view of the district's reluctance to provide bilingual instruction. In 1974 in New York, the consent decree in *Aspira* v. *Board of Education*[30] resulted in one of the largest bilingual programs in the country.

In *Keyes* v. *School District No. 1*,[31] the Supreme Court for the first time upheld a district court decision that placed Hispanic students under the broad category of "minority." This was most significant as it affected school desegregation cases in cities with multiethnic populations, especially where a third group was "numerically significant" enough to be considered separately in devising court-ordered remedies. In a subsequent decision in *Keyes*,[32] the court of appeals established that, when the two come in conflict, desegregation takes precedence over bilingual education. However, the court also appeared to endorse the concept that "a meaningful desegregation plan" must help Hispanic school children to reach the proficiency in English necessary to learn other basic subjects since, on remand, it ordered that evidence be brought forth to clarify the extent of need for children with limited English-language skills.

Perhaps the best known decision pertaining to the educational needs of children in public schools who have limited or no English-language skills is *Lau* v. *Nichols*. While this decision did not explicitly endorse bilingual education (or any other method of instruction), since this was not part of the evidence in the case, many groups and individuals considered the suit a major victory in the struggle to obtain equal educational opportunity through bilingual education. The court declared that providing the same instructional service to children with limited English skills did not provide equal educational opportunity to those children; based on civil rights law, the court further stated that school districts had to take "affirmative steps" to remedy the situation.

The *Lau* v. *Nichols* decision had significant impact also on state legislatures mandating or allowing bilingual instruction in public schools.[33] In 1971, motivated by the example set by Congress, Massachusetts had become the first state to pass legislation which mandated school districts with twenty or more children of limited English ability to provide transitional bilingual education programs. Other states quickly followed Massachusetts's example, and transitional bilingual education legislation, mandatory or simply permissive, was enacted in Texas, California, Illinois, Michigan, and many other states. State funds were thus added to federal monies, and the push for expansion of bilingual education was well on its way.

The first attempt to introduce legislation dealing with bilingual bicultural education in Wisconsin came in the spring of 1974. Proposed bilingual legislation (Senate Bill 747) died in committee that summer. In the fall of 1974 a coalition of Hispanic educators obtained the support of an influential legislator to assist in sponsoring and promoting a bill. In February, 1975, Senate Bill 126 was introduced by Senator Henry Dorman of Racine. Soon after, a similar bill was introduced in the assembly by Representative Joseph Czerwinski of Milwaukee. Several months of intensive lobbying followed, during which time the original bill was subjected to numerous amendments. In March, 1976, the bill was narrowly approved by the assembly and signed into law by the governor in May. For the first time in the history of the state, a law had been passed at the urging of Hispanic communities through-out Wisconsin to address the needs of thousands of children in need of adequate educational programs. State funding was provided. The CWBBAC played an important role in the final stages of lobbying for the legislation.

In early 1975, while Federal District Court Judge John W. Reynolds pondered his decision in the Milwaukee desegregation case, several events took place which are interesting because they reveal the degree of involve-ment as well as the growing sophistication of the CWBBAC. First, two members of the Board of Directors of the Milwaukee Public Schools re-signed and left vacancies to be filled. Recognizing that the balance of power on the board lay with these two individuals, the CWBBAC, following a series of caucuses with community groups and organizations throughout Milwaukee and subsequent efforts to obtain the support of several board members, came forth with a qualified Hispanic candidate for one of the vacancies. Intense political maneuvering ensued, but the effort proved to be unsuccessful. The board's conservative majority, anxious to solidify its power base, appointed two relatively unknown candidates of conservative orientation who had done poorly in the previous school board elections. It was evident that the board's majority had identified the Hispanic candidate with the "liberals" on the board and feared a takeover. A major Hispanic student walkout was staged under the leadership of the CWBBAC parents to protest the School Board's actions. Though not powerful enough to sway the board, the Hispanic community clearly was beginning to make itself heard and its priorities recognized. Its own cohesion, visibility, and sophisti-cation as a pressure group was growing.

In the Title VII (ESEA) proposal for 1975-1976, as a response to the CWBBAC's involvement in drafting the proposal, Milwaukee Public Schools requested that three new positions be funded—a parent coordinator and two assistants who would work on a regular basis with the CWBBAC and act as liaison between the administration and the group. The importance of these appointments must be stressed since it allowed the CWBBAC, which had been functioning for almost two years in an unstructured manner, to become organized and establish itself on a more solid footing. In September 1975, after much acrimonious discussion by the board about the controversial candidate recommended by the parents, who previously had been an active community organizer, the bilingual parent coordinator was appointed, and he quickly set out to finalize the structuring of the com-mittee. The fact that he was, prior to the appointment, a leader among the CWBBAC's parents facilitated his task and ensured support by most parents and Hispanic community organizations.

Immediately after the parent coordinator's office was established, the CWBBAC prepared a work agenda for the coming year. Its work in the community led most Hispanic leaders to realize the potential effects that desegregation could have on bilingual gains. By the end of 1975, they had done some background work on the issues. Furthermore, efforts by govern-mental agencies (like the Office for Civil Rights) to enforce Lau v. Nichols[34] also added to the CWBBAC's continual activity in demanding a *Lau* survey and a plan for compliance with the Supreme Court's decision. In a series of community meetings throughout the city, the CWBBAC succeeded in bringing to the attention of Hispanic and other parents the need for Milwaukee schools to comply with *Lau,* and a complaint was filed with the Office for Civil Rights. It was not until 1978 that OCR acted on this complaint and a compliance plan was developed in 1979. Expanding bilingual services, as well as understanding and preparing for desegregation were the goals of CWBBAC during the critical period preceding the court desegregation order.

To broaden the understanding of desegregation and its potential effects on bilingual education, initial contacts were made with attorneys from the Mexican American Legal Defense and Education Fund (MALDEF) in San Francisco and the Puerto Rican Legal Defense and Education Fund (PRLDEF) in New York regarding their handling of desegregation/bilingual cases in other cities. Other authorities on bilingual education throughout the country were also consulted. By the end of the year, the CWBBAC had completed its organizational work and was ready to move forward with additional resources and capabilities to promote equal opportunities for Hispanic students and teachers. The timing could not have been more appropriate.

A Year of Decision—1975

1975 was a year of activity and change for Milwaukee's schools. Three factors accounted for this: (1) an interdistrict desegregation plan was proposed in the state legislature; (2) a new superintendent of schools was hired; and (3) a decision by the federal court in the desegregation case appeared imminent.

In January State Representative Dennis Conta, in an effort to promote equality of educational opportunity in the city's schools, unveiled a plan under which a new school district would be created by merging two affluent suburban school districts (Whitefish Bay and Shorewood) with two high school clusters on the east side of the city.[35] Declaring segregated schools to be "not simply a 'Black problem' or a 'city problem,' " Representative Conta stressed that although Wisconsin did not have a state desegregation law as did neighboring Minnesota, Illinois, and Michigan, a lack of action was not necessarily justified. His plan documented declining state aid for education going to the city of Milwaukee in spite of higher costs in urban areas.

The Conta plan eventually went to the state assembly as a legislative proposal that was much discussed in the communities potentially affected by it, mostly school districts within Milwaukee County. There was great opposition to the proposal. However, once the suburbs were assured that they would not be absorbed into a metropolitan desegregation plan, but that incentives for voluntary transfer of some students would be provided, positive votes were forthcoming from their legislators. When the new Milwaukee school superintendent, Lee R. McMurrin, arrived in the summer, he helped to explain and was generally supportive of the Conta bill. Such legislation would surely help if the court were to find that Milwaukee's schools were segregated. Thus, McMurrin held many meetings with educators in the suburbs and publicly endorsed the idea of a student-transfer plan between the city and suburban schools.

The version of the Conta plan that finally passed the legislature later in 1976 provided financial incentives in addition to transportation costs for voluntary interdistrict transfers but did not change school district lines. Transportation costs were to be paid by the state for intracity transfers as well, if such transfers would produce greater desegregation. Chapter 220 (Wisconsin Statutes), as the legislation was later called, would become a major source of financial support for implementing Milwaukee's desegregation plan during 1976 and subsequent years.

While the transfer plan and the magnet schools (see pp. 18-19 for description of these schools), coupled with additional state monies, provided positive incentives for more Whites to participate in desegregation, they did not really produce "metropolitanism" nor did they give equal weight to the concerns of the minority students' parents. Blacks had many doubts about the transfer plan and feared that the best minority students would leave the city. Magnet schools, they also argued, had not produced much desegregation elsewhere and usually required Blacks to move out of newly formed schools with new programs to make room for Whites. As for Hispanics, since there were no bilingual programs in the suburbs but well-developed ones did exist in several schools in the city, it was unlikely that they would take advantage of the transfers in substantial numbers.

Later during desegregation planning in 1976, the Hispanic community and the CWBBAC suggested that a problem could evolve because of the discrepancy in the definitions given by Chapter 220 and those used in court deliberations. The first defined Hispanics as "minority" and the latter as "non-Black." Administration officials gave unclear information regarding the discrepancy as it could affect the intracity movement of Hispanics and other minority students seeking either bilingual or specialty programs. Chapter 220 proposed to pay for the transfer of minority students willing to attend city as well as suburban schools with a majority White population of 70 percent or more, or for White students to attend a school with a minority population of 70 percent or more. A minority student who attended a school already having a minority population of over 30 percent or more would not bring the school additional funds under the act.

The concern of the Hispanics was to gain some assurances as to how the needs of their children were to be addressed under desegregation. Students needing bilingual education could not be supported under this act if a school already had a 30 percent minority population. Would this mean that these students would not get the programs they needed? Hispanic educational issues were not seen as a major concern for school decision makers as they faced a court deciding a Black-White issue, although the implementation of any court ruling in Milwaukee would clearly have an impact on Hispanic children.

The Chapter 220 transfer plan continues to be implemented. There were 138 students transferring to Milwaukee from the suburbs on a full and part-time basis as of September 1979. A total of 1,054 students from both city and suburbs are involved in the program. Twelve out of eighteen suburbs have been involved in the program, and an independent citizen's council has been formed to aid implementation.

Some Whites and minorities benefit from new options available in desegregated settings. However, this kind of voluntary interdistrict transfer program is unlikely to have great impact in desegregating the schools, and it does not provide most Hispanic students with programs which take into account their desires and needs.

It is not surprising that a plan calling for an interdistrict solution to segregation was proposed in Milwaukee since the idea was raised elsewhere in the courts as well as in the political arena during the midseventies.[36] While each city is unique, as is each court case, the growing minority population and the unlikelihood of major changes in residential segregation make metropolitan solutions reasonable if any significant degree of desegregation is to occur.

New Superintendent McMurrin Takes the Initiative

In 1974 the superintendent of the Milwaukee schools resigned, and the system was under the direction of an acting superintendent until July, 1975. The search for a superintendent was difficult, given the various factions on the School Board and their respective views of the qualities desired of this key official. After much debate and some internal turmoil, the School Board narrowed the search down to two candidates. During interviews, the School Board questioned the candidates on their views about desegregation and its purpose and impact on the system. The conservative majority, its numbers boosted by the two handpicked conservative candidates who had filled the vacancies on the board, gave its support and approval to Lee R. McMurrin, whom they viewed as a moderate and, therefore, a stabilizing force for the district as it faced an impending desegregation order.

A man of boundless energy and a high level of enthusiasm and optimism, McMurrin literally took to the streets, making public appearances at every opportunity offered to him, and meeting with major civic groups in the city, with politicians, business and industry representatives, and with church groups—in sum, with anyone willing to listen to his views.

Immediately he set out to plan a general strategy to improve the system and expand opportunities for all students, based on concepts tried out in Toledo and Cincinnati. The preliminary steps toward formulating a broad policy statement which would commit the district to improved opportunities for all students were taken in the summer months. The result was the *Statement on Education and Human Rights,* which was adopted by the School Board on September 2, 1975. This document, which McMurrin developed and promoted, addressed current conditions in Milwaukee, especially in the schools where "not all persons are recipients of the rights and benefits afforded them as citizens of our state and nation." After recognizing the rich resources available to the schools in the city's multiethnic population, and the housing and socioeconomic barriers which had led to racial and ethnic separation of groups, the School Board pledged in the *Statement,* among other things, "to work toward a more integrated society and to enlist the support of individuals as well as that of groups and agencies, both private and governmental, in such an effort." It also included provisions which urged

17

"appropriate communication and action techniques to air and reduce the grievances of individuals and groups," and to review "all policies and practices of this school district in order to achieve . . . the objectives of this statement." Although general in its overall intent, the *Statement* did highlight some crucial concerns and placed the burden of bringing about change on the district. In addition to permitting the School Board to project a more positive image just before the court ruling was expected, the document gave the new superintendent a chance at the outset of his term of office to work towards consensus, to attempt to build a voluntary plan for desegregation, and to muster broad-based public support.

In October the second of McMurrin's major initiatives was unveiled in a series of proposals for expanded options for students at all levels. These bore the titles of *High Schools Unlimited* (Senior High), *Schools for the Transition* (Junior High), and *Options for Learning* (Elementary).

High Schools Unlimited would make it possible for Milwaukee students to take courses not regularly offered at their own high schools at other schools on a part-time basis. Schools would be "paired" so as to enhance ethnic/racial "mixing," usually a predominantly Black school matched with a predominantly White one. In addition, satellite centers were proposed as part of the plans, and a career specialty would be added to each high school. Transportation between two cooperating schools would be provided by the district.

Schools for the Transition for the junior high level was so named because "children undergo a rapid personal transition in the interval between elementary school and senior high school."[37] The middle or junior high schools would offer alternatives in education to attract pupils city-wide. An example given by the administration was Jackie Robinson School, an alternative open classroom program which already existed.

Options for Learning addressed the elementary school level. The proposal called for establishing alternative elementary schools devoted to different learning approaches. Parents would choose voluntarily to send their children, and ethnic mixing would be considered when selecting the students for the program. Some of the proposed programs (many of which were established) were: open education schools, Montessori schools, basic fundamental schools, a second-language proficiency school (German), schools for the gifted and talented, schools for the creative arts; there even was talk of a bilingual school, a concept that later was changed to "bilingual centers" or schools with bilingual program components.[38] The Jefferson Teacher-Pupil Learning Center opened in September 1975 as a city-wide elementary school and set a model for other city-wide specialty schools.

The new program proposals constituted a reform effort for the entire school system in order to calm the apprehension of many Whites about possible desegregation efforts. In reality, these reforms were based on existing efforts within the district; the innovation was due mostly to a redirection of effort and a new focus of attention. McMurrin knew how to use existing community organizations and communications networks to encourage the public to accept educational change. Assisted by some of the liberal board members and the recently formed Community and Advisory Group Relations Committee,[39] he submitted to the board his *Recommendations for the Proposed Involvement Structure for Alternative School Planning and Integration.* This plan would eventually facilitate the formation of the Committee of 100, which will be discussed later in more detail. Much credit should be given to community-based organizations which had struggled for years for quality education and in meeting after meeting pressured the board to take action on the proposed plans.[41] It was the work of these people that paved the way for more input by minority group organizations.

Throughout the year and into 1976 McMurrin continued to project a positive image of himself and the school system in order to allay the fears of many, to create a supportive climate, and to be ready to propose positive remedies to the court, should a finding of illegal segregation be made against the district.

The Court Order:
Illegal Segregation in Milwaukee Schools

On January 19, 1976, Judge John W. Reynolds, Chief Judge for the Eastern District of Wisconsin, issued a lengthy decision in *Armstrong* v. *O'Connell* (C.A. No. 65-C-173). The lawsuit had been filed originally in June, 1965, but the trial itself did not begin until September 10, 1973, (at which time the NAACP attorneys withdrew from the case)[42] and lasted through the end of the year. Reynolds, who had waited more than a year before ruling on the case, was forceful and direct in finding the school system unconstitutionally segregated:

> I have concluded that segregation exists in the Milwaukee Public Schools and that this segregation was intentionally created and maintained by the defendants. Such segregation is violative of the equal protection of the laws guaranteed to all Americans by the Fourteenth Amendment and cannot lawfully be allowed to continue. I shall accordingly order that the Milwaukee School System be integrated; that the defendants forthwith begin the formulation of plans to effectively achieve that goal; and that a Master be appointed to make recommendations to the court with respect to the question of an appropriate remedy.[43]

Dr. John A. Gronouski, former Tax Commissioner of Wisconsin, Postmaster General, and United States Ambassador to Poland, and Dean of the LBJ School of Public Affairs at the University of Texas at Austin, was appointed Special Master. He was instructed by the court to assist in the development of a plan to desegregate the Milwaukee Public School System. In addition to his knowledge about Wisconsin, his wealth of political experience, and his ethnic background in a city with a significant population of Polish extraction, Gronouski was a trusted friend of Reynolds, who was relying on him to skillfully guide the district's efforts in formulating a plan.

21

Reynolds's faith in Gronouski was not misplaced as his actions would prove over almost two years of his tenure as Special Master.

In addition, Reynolds ruled that the suit should be treated as a "class action" since the forty-one plaintiffs, who were Black and White children, represented a larger group, namely all school-age children who were deprived of an equal education. The judge appointed a well-known Milwaukee attorney, Irvin B. Charne, to represent the interests of the unnamed class members. Lloyd Barbee, the original attorney for the plaintiffs, had labored alone for years in spite of his additional duties as a state representative and as a lawyer engaged in private practice, and could not be expected to continue in this case all by himself. The work load was expected to increase substantially since the decision was likely to be appealed by the School Board. Barbee and Charne soon developed a cooperative working relationship and were able immediately to take on the tasks which lay ahead of them.

In his decision and order, Judge Reynolds discussed various facts and policies which, in his judgment, showed that the School Board was knowingly and willfully operating a segregated school system. As in many school desegregation cases, the evidence included areas such as boundary changes, facilities (including additions to schools), intact busing, student transfer policies, personnel practices related to hiring and assigning minority teachers to minority schools, special programs, and financial expenditures. The major findings included the following:

1. The Milwaukee School Board dealt with overcrowding in predominantly Black schools located in areas previously inhabited by Whites by changing school boundaries which simply moved Black children into adjacent areas.

2. School additions or portable classrooms were provided to alleviate overcrowding in Black areas, rather than adjusting boundaries into generally White areas.

3. New schools were consistently built in newer districts, which were White residential areas.

4. In those cases where Black children were bused, busing was on an "intact" basis; that is, classes of Black children bused were kept intact in their new schools.

5. Even when the School Board attempted to provide the freedom to attend the school of one's choice through the transfer plan, segregation was encouraged; White parents viewed and used the transfer plan as an open invitation to leave predominantly Black schools. School Board testimony did not argue that such action had indeed been taken. They did argue that all School Board decisions dealing with site selection, school construction, additions and renovations, boundary lines and intact busing were made in such a manner to retain the concept of the neighborhood school, and not to foster segregation.

6. The Board consistently refused to take any action to lessen the degree of racial segregation which resulted from residential patterns and the neighborhood school policy as modified by the free and open transfer policies.[44]

Relying heavily on the United States Supreme Court's decision in *Keyes*, Reynolds stated: "The law is not blind as to only proscribe school segregation which is the result of legislative enactments bearing on their face the mark of governmental action violative of the Equal Protection Clause of the Fourteenth Amendment. The law equally forbids more subtle means of achieving the proscribed end of governmental segregation on the basis of race. The facially neutral actions of state authorities constitute illegal and unconstitutional *de jure* segregation if they are intended to and have the effect of racial separation."[45]

In analyzing the evidence, the judge found that the district had seemingly "reasonable and at times educationally necessary" explanations for their policies and actions. But he went on to reject them, based on their cumulative effect:

> In and of itself, any one act or practice may not indicate a segregative intent, but when considered together and over an extended period of time, they do. These acts, previously described in detail, constituted a consistent and deliberate policy of racial isolation and segregation for a period of twenty years. It is hard to believe that out of all the decisions made by the school authorities under varying conditions over a twenty-year period, mere chance resulted in there being no decision that resulted in the furthering of integration.[46]

The court dismissed rather harshly the arguments put forth by the defendants and reached the following conclusions:

> The fact that substantial segregation was considered by the school authorities to be educationally necessary and a prerequisite to quality education does not make it legal. The Constitution does not guarantee one a quality education; it guarantees one an equal education, and the law in this country is that a segregated education that is mandated by school authorities is inherently unequal.
>
> The Court concludes that the defendants have knowingly carried out a systematic program of segregation affecting all of the city's students, teachers, and school facilities, and have intentionally brought about and maintained a dual school system. The court therefore holds that the entire Milwaukee public school system is unconstitutionally segregated.[47]

As is often the case, the court did not provide any guidelines or place any limitations upon the remedial options which were open to the parties and the Special Master.

Public reaction to the decision was mixed. The board's conservatives decried the injustice perpetrated against them by the court and promised to appeal to the highest court, if needed, to overturn the decision. The liberal faction, which included the three Black members, hailed it as the vindication of a long struggle to achieve equal educational opportunity and urged the entire board and the administration to get on with the work which lay ahead. Politicians generally remained silent, but some did issue public statements about the decisions, both positive and negative. The mayor stressed the need to abide by the law. The media gave extensive coverage to the issues, and the analyses were mostly objective and tempered with moderation.

Planning for Desegregation

As the planning for desegregation developed, Hispanics took advantage of opportunities to participate in formal structures as well as to use the media to make their views heard. They shared with other community groups the frustrations involved in trying to fashion a plan for a board which insisted exclusively on voluntary desegregation. Nevertheless, the process did enable Hispanics to influence others in the community and Special Master Gronouski as well.

The process of developing a plan to desegregate Milwaukee's public schools would rely on two structures: (1) the Special Master's office which included Gronouski's assistant, John Gilligan; and (2) the Committee of 100, a broadly representative community group. Soon after he arrived in Milwaukee, Gronouski emphasized that he wanted the planning process to be open so that a broad cross section of opinion could be heard. He met with dozens of groups to explain his role and obtain their input into the desegregation planning process. In this activity he was assisted by John Gilligan, who knew the community well.

The Committee of 100 was created by the administration and the board in accord with their previous commitments to provide for citizen involvement in the desegregation process. Immediately after the court order, elections were held in every school cluster to select parent and staff representatives to sit on this city-wide committee. Local businesses, governmental agencies, and established citizen and religious groups were asked for representation, on technical, nonvoting subcommittees. The idea was to create a committee of 100 members, including the administration's representatives. (The actual number was closer to 125.) The Committee of 100, as it became known, would be the principal vehicle to channel community and parent input into the desegregation planning process, as well as the development of the plan(s). The schools were divided into twelve geographic areas, each containing ten elementary schools whose combined racial makeup was approximately 35 to 45 percent Black. League Planning Councils representing these areas, with the Junior High Council and Senior High Council, made up the Fourteen-League Planning Council. The League Planning Councils would recommend to the Committee of 100 which would, in turn, recommend to the administration and board.

The CWBBAC felt that it was important to get Hispanics elected to the Committee of 100 so that their specific concerns would be heard and acted on. By spring of 1976, the Committee of 100 was well established and did include four Hispanics. Its timetable for completion of assigned tasks was very tight, and regular weekly meetings (and often even more frequent meetings) were required. The Hispanic members of the Committee of 100 became the spokespersons for the Hispanic community's concerns over the potential effect desegregation would have on existing bilingual programs. They could also monitor the impact of desegregation on a much larger group, the Hispanic students not enrolled in bilingual programs. The role of sensitizing the Committee of 100 to the educational needs and aspirations of Hispanics fell on these four individuals and their alternates, who were constantly assisted by the counsel and investigative work of the CWBBAC's parent coordinator, as well as several professional and nonprofessional volunteers who worked along with him. The influence of these individuals extended beyond the formal planning process and was exercised at many informal meetings with board members, administrators, and community groups. It was a time of trying to influence as many people as possible to assure recognition of Hispanic needs as part of the plan which was primarily seen as remedying a Black-White issue.

Following his appointment, Gronouski developed procedures for receiving input from various groups and organizations. He held a series of community public hearings, one of which took place in April in the near south side's Hispanic neighborhood. Representatives of the CWBBAC and other interested persons attended in force and urged the Master to recognize the needs of Hispanic students and their rights under federal and state law. The Hispanic community was uncertain about what would happen. Gronouski listened but promised only to study the matter carefully. A series of meetings with parent groups followed in which CWBBAC representatives explained what had happened. The parents were given the opportunity to express their fears and apprehensions, as well as to make suggestions on how to proceed. As a follow-up to these sessions, in a long letter to Gronouski dated April 26, the CWBBAC issued its first position paper on desegregation/integration and added observations and recommendations relative to "Hispano pupil enrollment." The group came out unequivocally in favor of desegregation but wary of the means of implementation being considered, which included the possible reassignment and dispersal of many students with potentially devastating impact on the bilingual bicultural program.[48] The CWBBAC asked for a better definition of what a desegregated school was, and recommended that Hispanic schools be considered desegregated, provided the minority ratios given by the court were met. The CWBBAC also alerted the Master to the new obligations that the district would have once state bilingual legislation was signed into law (which had been approved by the legislature in March). Finally, it mentioned for the first time there might be a need to formally intervene in the case to protect the rights of Hispanic pupils.

By late spring the planning process was underway but no official recognition of the needs of Hispanic students had come forth from Gronouski's office or the administration, although the Committee of 100 passed various resolutions to highlight these special concerns. The Special Master's report to the court on progress made through May concentrated on teacher desegregation and plans for 1976-77, but did not mention Hispanics. The School Board was very reluctant to design any involuntary desegregation program; rather it opted to develop an alternative voluntary plan, which was eventually submitted to the court in late May. In view of these facts, the CWBBAC began to question the adequacy of its strategy of cooperation and started to explore other possible avenues.

Early in June, a meeting was held by some members of the CWBBAC and other Hispanics with Lloyd Barbee and a representative from Irvin Charne's office, to sound out their opinion on a possible CWBBAC intervention. Barbee explained that he would not object to such a motion, but rather would see it as a friendly move. No firm decision was reached by the CWBBAC on this matter for several weeks. The CWBBAC was sure of what should *not* be allowed to happen (i.e., the destruction of the bilingual programs), but it was not convinced about the necessity to intervene at that time. In addition, CWBBAC lacked the resources needed to intervene, even with the assistance of MALDEF and PRLDEF, both of which insisted on a local attorney handling most of the preparatory work as well as the continuing work after filing, including necessary court appearances. Thus, it was decided to forego the intervention approach. Instead, the CWBBAC opted to further attempt to influence the planning process to ensure the protection of Hispanic students.[49] There would not be much time for this approach because the plan which the School Board submitted was rejected on June 11 by the court as unworkable and Judge Reynolds issued an order requiring Milwaukee Public Schools to file a student desegregation plan with the court by June 30. The plan, which would be reviewed by the Special Master, was to have a three-year time span, and schools would be considered desegregated only if they had ratios of 25 to 45 percent Black student enrollment.

The idea of fixed ratios of Black students in every school presented a potential problem for Hispanic students, in the CWBBAC's view. In another letter to the Special Master dated June 30, the group expressed grave concern about the possibility of schools being desegregated strictly along Black-White ratios, with Hispanic students classified as "non-Black" for student assignment purposes. In urging that Hispanics be considered a distinct racial/ethnic minority for desegregation planning, the group was trying to avoid the possibility of schools being desegregated by combining Blacks and Hispanics (classified as Whites), as had occurred in some Texas cities in the early seventies.[50] This was clearly a critical time, and the court still did not recognize Hispanics as a distinct group for desegregation planning. It was then that the idea of drafting a statement for submission to the administration and the School Board was conceived. The statement would spell out some safeguards in the desegregation plan for Hispanic students.

In the first draft of the *Statement of Assurances*, the CWBBAC alerted the administration and Gronouski to the contradiction involved in the dual classification of Hispanic students ("non-Black" under the court order and "minority" under Chapter 220) and the financial impact the discrepancy in definition could have on the district. Hispanic parents legitimately feared that schools with predominantly Hispanic populations (where most bilingual programs were in effect) would suffer excessive removal of Hispanics to allow for the required 25 percent minimum of Blacks:

> If a school is already 30% Hispanic, then the transportation of Black children assigned to such schools *cannot* be covered by the state. Hispanic and Blacks are both "minority." On the other hand, in order to have a minimum of 25% Black in every school, you could only allow for 5% Hispanic and other minority. You would then be displacing one minority by another.[51]

But, on July 9, the court approved the plan developed by Milwaukee Public Schools and the ratios recommended by the Special Master with the provision that one-third of the schools be desegregated yearly as per the original time span. No mention of the Hispanic concerns appeared in this order.

The CWBBAC was very disturbed since neither the administration nor the Special Master considered the existing legal precedents related to the treatment of Hispanics during desegregation. The importance of *United States v. Texas Education Agency*[52] and *Keyes*[53] pertaining to a third ethnic group during desegregation implementation had been completely ignored.

Assurances and Broken Promises

The attention of the community now needed to be focused on implementation procedures. The CWBBAC spent the balance of the summer developing and negotiating with the administration a document to be formally presented to the School Board in early fall that would delineate a set of principles for the treatment of Hispanics during desegregation implementation. In mid-September the paper was sent to the board's Committee on Instruction where it was discussed at length after Hispanic parents and leaders presented arguments in its favor. On October 5 it was approved by the board with the endorsement of the conservative faction while the three Black board members voted "present." It was obvious to the CWBBAC that the conservative support was due to the fact that under these principles much less movement of students would be required, especially in the schools with heavy Hispanic populations, most of which were located in the near south side, which was a White-Hispanic area. By using Hispanics who were already there to desegregate those schools, there would be no need to bus Black children in from the predominantly Black north side of town.

The Black board members regarded this as a ploy by the conservative faction to lessen the impact of the desegregation plan and, in spite of several private meetings and generally good relations with the CWBBAC before the issue was raised, they could not bring themselves to vote with the very same persons with whom they had consistently struggled to promote a meaningful desegregation plan. They did not want to appear anti-Hispanic by voting "No" on the motion so they voted "present," which was tantamount to abstaining. The local press quoted one Black school board member as saying she "could not support letting Latins become part of the desegregation plan if they would not accept the possibility of being transferred to another school," while another expressed her inability to "support special treatment for any group."[54] The basic problem involved trust (or the lack of it); it has occurred in other desegregation situations because emphasis has been placed on desegregation along Black-White lines and because school boards have had a history of resisting desegregation, thus making Blacks very suspicious of their actions. Cooperative efforts among Blacks and Hispanics are made very difficult in this situation, which ultimately strengthens resistance to any educational change for the benefit of minorities.

Nonetheless, the statement, titled *Major Issues, Assurances, and Legal Principles Affecting the Hispanic Pupil during Desegregation Efforts* (also called the *Statement of Assurances*), committed the board to the following:

1. Hispanic pupils need to be considered an ethnic/racial minority group and an identifiable class, forming part of the "minority group pupil" population of the Milwaukee Public School System.

2. The combined numbers of "minority group pupils" shall be kept within the ratios set by the court order.

3. Schools with Hispanic pupil enrollment constituting most or all of the minority pupil population shall be considered desegregated if the percentage of minority pupils fall within those set by the court.[55]

Other provisions pertained to the newly-approved Wisconsin Bilingual Bicultural Education Act, pupil transportation, program options, and the status of teachers in existing and contemplated bilingual bicultural education programs. The latter had been an issue of much concern for the CWBBAC and bilingual teachers. There had been no clear criteria for the treatment of bilingual and Hispanic teachers during desegregation nor was there, at this time, state certification for them.[56] Bilingual programs could not be implemented unless bilingual teachers were assigned to schools with significant numbers of children needing these programs.

As required by the board's action of October 5, the *Statement of Assurances* was forwarded to the court and the plaintiffs' attorneys on October 22 by board attorney Lawrence Hammond. In his accompanying letter, he also informed the court of the board's intentions of planning desegregation for Phase II and III along "minority lines," as opposed to simply in "Black" terms.

On October 28 a directive *Principal Co-Captains for Phase II Planning for the*

1976-1977 School Year was sent to the League Planning Councils instructing them as follows:

> For the purposes of league planning for Phase II and Phase III, the following students are to be considered a minority along with Black students in all efforts to racially balance a school.
>
> American Indian or Alaskan Native
> Asian or Pacific Islander
> Hispanic (Spanish Surname)[57]

At last there seemed to be the language to ensure Hispanic students some protection in what was previously a strictly Black-White plan. However, on November 17 Lloyd Barbee and Irvin Charne wrote to board attorney Lawrence Hammond objecting to paragraphs 1 through 3 on the grounds that "the policies and principles contained in . . . the statement attached to your letter are contrary to previous orders of the court and are, therefore, unacceptable." Their letter went on to explain that ". . . this case from its inception has involved the issue of unconstitutional segregation of Black and White pupils. The issue of unconstitutional segregation of Hispanic pupils has not been litigated in this action." After referring to the original decision (January 1976) and the June 11 order, they added: "Substituting Hispanic pupils for Black pupils in determining whether a school population meets the twenty-five percent to forty-five percent ratio is, in our view, contrary to the court's order. . . . We do feel that desegregation of Hispanic students is desirable and can be achieved without deviating from the court imposed ratio." Finally, they expressed a need to review the plan which the administration was preparing to submit in December before offering any "alternative plans for desegregating Hispanic pupils which are consistent with the plan for desegregating the White and Black student population."

Although they appeared to be legally correct in their position visa-à-vis the status of Hispanic students against whom no constitutional violations had been found, Barbee and Charne's position was a blow to the CWBBAC's plans. It appeared as if Barbee was backtracking on his previous statements of support for the concerns of Hispanics and that Charne, who was the court-appointed attorney for the unnamed class which included Hispanic students under the broad category of "White," concurred with him. How then could the interests of Hispanic students be entrusted to Mr. Charne?

Once again, the possibility of intervention surfaced in the CWBBAC's discussions of this new development, but no action was decided upon. The resources to initiate and maintain a legal action were nonexistent, and the CWBBAC was still working to ensure that the board's plan would include the *Statement of Assurances* as official policy, at least until the court, upon reviewing the plan, ruled on the issue. After all, the document had met with the approval of both Deputy Superintendent David Bennett, who was the key administrator in charge of desegregation planning, and the School Board itself. More importantly, the Special Master himself had recognized that special consideration should be accorded to certain students. In his November 15 report to the court, he recommended general criteria which should be followed by the School Board in developing the desegregation plan to be submitted to the court in early January 1977. Criterion 6 read as follows:

> In accordance with a suggestion of the Superintendent of Education, the plan adopted should accommodate the special needs of non-Black students who are of Hispanic, and Native-American origin, students who qualify for Title I programs, and who have exceptional needs. Specific plans for these students should be an *integral part* of the desegregation plan to be presented to the court on January 3, 1977.[58]

Apparently the constant flow of information from the CWBBAC to Gronouski's office had succeeded in convincing him to give Hispanic and other students special attention. With such strong support, perhaps Barbee and Charne's position would not prevail. But new developments were in the making which would radically change the CWBBAC's perceptions of how the planning process was proceeding and force it to consider more drastic measures in the struggle for equal educational opportunity for the school system's second largest minority.

Unexpected Developments

December of 1976 was a hectic month for those involved in desegregation planning in Milwaukee. It was particularly frustrating for the Committee of 100 and the CWBBAC. Nonetheless, citizen involvement grew considerably in response to the conservative faction of the Milwaukee School Board's defiance of the court and the recommendations of the citizen committee they had created.

On December 8 the superintendent released a draft of the *Comprehensive Plan*[59] for Phase II of desegregation which included many of the recommendations made by the League Planning Councils and the Committee of 100. It was the plan that later the Special Master would speak of as the "community's plan." Thanks to the efforts of the Hispanic members of the committee, it included a component that promised an expansion of existing bilingual programs from twelve to twenty-four schools at a cost of approximately three-quarters of a million dollars. It also included the complete text of the *Statement of Assurances*. While the thrust of the plan was mostly voluntary desegregation using magnet and specialty school incentives, there were backup mandatory clauses that would ensure compliance with the required two-thirds desegregated schools by September 1977. It received broad support from most segments of the community, governmental agencies, and the media.

The board's conservatives were firm in resisting any plan that would involve involuntary movement of students. Advised by their attorneys about the opinion in the Supreme Court's decision in the Austin case,[60] they amended the *Comprehensive Plan* and had Hammond prepare another plan for submission on January 3, 1977, the deadline set by the court. The essence of their argument was that Milwaukee's neighborhoods did not become racially segregated because of any governmental action and that the School Board based its student assignments on neighborhoods.[61] The *Milwaukee-Austin Plan* (as it was named) called for the partial desegregation of predominantly Black schools that had been identified by Reynolds as evidence of actual constitutional violations. Upon approving their plan, they called on the superintendent to use his publicity machinery to muster public support for it. The superintendent followed the dictates of the board, and much confusion resulted. The board thought that they would avoid the anger of the court if something with more substance was prepared and submitted as well. After amending the *Comprehensive Plan* by deleting all involuntary student assignment clauses, they sent it to the court, without official endorsement, as a separate document titled *Memorandum in Response.*[62]

In terms of the effect on Hispanic students, these new developments led to more confusion and a greater lack of trust in the School Board and the superintendent. In mid-December the superintendent announced publicly he could not desegregate along "minority lines" as proposed in the *Comprehensive Plan.*[63] Once again, Hispanics would be considered with the "non-Black" student class. This was a retraction of the principles approved by the board earlier in the *Statement of Assurances.* To a great extent, this action prompted the Hispanic community's contemplated intervention plans. It was not clear why the administration, without board approval, withdrew the plans submitted to the court in the *Statement of Assurances* and attempted rather to include the concerns of the CWBBAC under a new legal concept called "test of reasonableness."

This approach suggested by Superintendent McMurrin was in essence an "escape valve" request, given the fact that with decreasing enrollment and increasing "minority" student populations it would be impossible to attempt the desegregation of Milwaukee Schools within the ratios given by the court in June. Under this "test of reasonableness" McMurrin intended to request exemptions of certain schools from the court's guidelines. Among these would be Hispanic-White schools, schools for special or exceptional educational services, and predominantly Black schools in stable integrated neighborhoods.

Apparently the superintendent thought he could satisfy the CWBBAC by claiming Hispanic-White schools as exemptions in the desegregation process, thus leaving the matter still primarily a Black-White issue only. But, the CWBBAC, although supportive in principle of the "test of reasonableness" approach, insisted that the status of Hispanics had to be well defined. In January 1977 the CWBBAC sought assistance and advice from attorneys and educators locally and throughout the country and on February 2, 1977 registered with the court a petition of intervention. That same week the Special Master held hearings on the plans presented by the defendants in January, but the CWBBAC was denied participation in them because it was not a party to the case.

Hispanics Move to Intervene

The CWBBAC's petition of intervention is an important set of documents to consider. Like similar requests in other desegregation cases, the attempt was to protect the rights of Hispanic children to bilingual education programs as opposed to having the court make a finding of discrimination against Hispanics. The CWBBAC knew that the Milwaukee Public School's proposed expansion of bilingual programs was actually a response to the newly enacted Bilingual Bicultural Education Act of Wisconsin[64] and to the pressures of the Hispanic community. The expansion, in their view, was not due to the good will of the board or the administration; therefore, it might not be carried out. Thus, to reaffirm its position and to underscore the need for compliance with the Bilingual Act and the *Lau* decision, the CWBBAC had to bring the issues and concerns it had raised before to other fronts. The court was obviously one of those. The reasoning of the CWBBAC was that a court endorsement of Hispanic claims would probably force the board to be more responsive and would also prevent unnecessary movement and dispersal of Hispanic students during the desegregation process.

In the intervention documents, the CWBBAC explained how classifying Hispanics as non-Black could result in the use of Hispanic students as White to desegregate predominantly Black schools where White parents would not volunteer to send their children. The council then asked the court to consider Hispanics a distinct ethnic/racial/minority group. It stressed that the use of Hispanic students as Whites to integrate Black schools was contrary to the very intent of desegregation and ignored how the principles set in *Brown* v. *Topeka* might also apply to Hispanics.[65] Finally, the CWBBAC argued that its main intent was to be allowed to participate in the court proceedings to ensure input by Hispanics in the final desegregation plan ordered by the court.

On February 15 and 16, the plaintiffs and the defendants submitted documents opposing the CWBBAC's request for intervention. Both parties argued that the intervention was untimely. The plaintiffs raised the same claims made previously in Barbee and Charne's letter of November 17, 1976, and suggested that the interests of Hispanic students were protected adequately through the provision for bilingual education programs under state statute. Furthermore, they argued, there had been no show of intent to dismantle or impair the bilingual programs by any of the parties involved. The plaintiffs' opposition in essence claimed that desegregation in Milwaukee was, because of legal requirements, a Black and White issue and that the Hispanics' intervention would only delay the process and would also water down the remedy sought, which aimed to correct only violations against Blacks. The defendants argued that the rights and concerns of Hispanic students were not in danger and that the board's approval of the *Statement of Assurances* by itself ensured the protection of such rights.

In its *Reply Memorandum*[66] to the opposition of the plaintiffs and defendants, the CWBBAC rebutted with both legal and educational arguments. It attempted to show the court that there were legal precedents that would allow for intervention in the proceedings and that the protection of the interests of Hispanic students could not be left to plaintiffs' attorneys who neither appeared to understand the claims of Hispanic parents nor were experienced in the theory and practice of bilingual education. It expressed regret over the plaintiffs' opposition.[67] In response to the defendants' arguments, it was granted that while Milwaukee had a progressive history regarding the offering of bilingual services, recent retractions by the administration and contradicting policies enacted as a result of desegregation could reduce concern for bilingual education, thus affecting the future expansion and improvement of the bilingual programs. Most importantly, the CWBBAC argued that Hispanic students could not depend for the protection of their rights on an institution that continued to default in its obligation to respect the rights of other minorities: "Intervenors' interest cannot be held to ride on the assurance of a party so derelict in protecting similar rights of (other) minority children."[68]

The CWBBAC's *Reply Memorandum* also dealt with the Special Master's report of February 17, 1977.[69] This report contained Gronouski's recommendations to the court based on the hearings held the first week of the same month. The document was a considerable departure from his previous reports because it proposed to change the strict percentages set earlier in regard to Black student populations per school. Gronouski was now proposing that by September 1977, the Milwaukee Public Schools had to be desegregated so that two-thirds of all schools would have Black student populations between 25 and 40 percent, one-sixth of all schools with Black populations between 20 and 65 percent, and the remaining one-sixth with Black populations between 15 and 75 percent. The report was very critical of the School Board, calling the *Memorandum in Response* "no plan at all" and the *Milwaukee-Austin Plan* "a blatant defiance of the court order."

In effect, Gronouski had given specificity to the administration's request for a "test of reasonableness." Rather than give them a carte blanche in terms of schools to be exempted from the ratios or to limit exemptions to specific schools, his recommendation provided the necessary flexibility which the Milwaukee Public Schools was asking for. Moreover, the compromise ratios were something the plaintiffs could live with since they guaranteed desegregation at the original ratios (25 to 45 percent Black) in a significant portion of the district. It appeared that the remaining third of the schools with ratios of 20 to 65 percent Black and 15 to 75 percent Black would accommodate the most highly segregated schools and reduce the movement of students. Hispanic students, of course, would benefit from the use of the "escape valves."

The CWBBAC was most concerned with section 1 (e) of the recommendations which made reference to Hispanic students:

> Nothing in this order is intended to prevent the Superintendent from designating Hispanic students, Native Americans and other minority students as separate minority populations and according them priority over other non-Black students in assignment to schools with programs designed to meet their special needs.[70]

This clause represented the most direct and significant acknowledgement regarding Hispanic students made up to that moment in the Milwaukee desegregation process. And it was evident that Gronouski was, at least in principle, agreeing with the CWBBAC's contentions. However, the clause was permissive and not a mandate. The Hispanic community proceeded to request that the clause be incorporated in the expected final desegregation order and made mandatory.

With the *Reply Memorandum* the CWBBAC included a *Critique of the Desegregation Plans before the Special Master*[71] and gave an extensive rationale and examples as to the possible effects of the plans on Hispanic students. In that document, they insisted on mandatory provisions requiring Milwaukee schools to protect the rights of Hispanics to bilingual programs and to assure equitable treatment in the event that involuntary movement of students became necessary.

In spite of the events described above, by this time the Hispanic community was extremely disappointed with the total treatment it had received in the desegregation process. Within the community itself there were considerable discussions and some animosity toward the various parties. The CWBBAC had maintained continual pressure on the court and the school district. However, in its involvement in the legal and bureaucratic process, it neglected to negotiate with other Hispanic groups and, to a degree, disregarded the scattered opposition to desegregation that was emerging among certain bilingual teachers in the district. Leaders of teacher groups were worried about the possible effects the final order might have on them. The problem was further complicated by their realization that bilingual certification standards were being prepared by the State Department of Public Instruction, and the CWBBAC had taken a hard line against the "grandfather-clausing" of bilingual teachers on the job, by suggesting that teachers be required to show competency prior to their licensing as bilingual teachers.[72] In an unpredicted move, certain teachers shared with students their perceptions of the desegregation process and how it would damage bilingual education in Milwaukee. They considered the CWBBAC's involvement in desegregation to be misguided. This viewpoint caused Hispanic students at a local high school to stage a walkout and to picket the court proceedings. For the first time it seemed as if the Hispanic community was split on the issue of desegregation. In reality it was a small incident that did not have significant impact on the legal claims made by the CWBBAC. The court had already announced that it would hear the motion of intervention on March 25, 1977.

Subsequent to his February 17 report, Gronouski received, in response to his package, briefs from the plaintiffs, defendants, the teacher association, and the CWBBAC (through its *Reply Memorandum*). The superintendent of schools had personally reacted to the report calling its guidelines rigid and impossible to comply with if adopted by the court. Thus, Gronouski prepared another set of recommendations which he submitted to the court on March 7.[73] In these recommendations, he maintained the Black student ratios he proposed in February but required that by September 1977 only another fifty-four schools be desegregated. He did, however, elaborate on Superintendent McMurrin's "test of reasonableness" concept calling it "vague in definition and indeterminate in application." Again he made reference to the Hispanics and argued that the exemptions to the court's requirements claimed by Milwaukee Schools could be implemented by the administration by using the new percentages for desegregation he recommended in the February report. Gronouski referred to the *Statement of Assurances* and said that those schools with a high concentration of Hispanic students could be considered desegregated if space were provided for a minimum of 15 to 20 percent Black students:

> Moreover, while the ranges set forth in Recommendation 1 (b) of my report are defined in terms of Black student ratios, there is sufficient flexibility to permit the school administration to utilize in almost all cases its preferred minority student ratio desegregation criteria. As stated in Recommendation 1 (e) of my Report, there is nothing in the Report's remedial recommendations that prevents school officials from assigning Hispanic or other minority students to schools with programs designed to meet their special needs, and designating those schools as among the ones with 15 or 20 percent Black student populations.[74]

On March 17 Judge Reynolds issued what was supposed to have been his final desegregation order.[75] The order reaffirmed Gronouski's earlier recommendations to the court of both February 17 and March 7, 1977. A second part of the order was a set of appendixes which were amended excerpts from the so-called *Green Plan* (the *Comprehensive Plan* prepared by the administration and the community). A very important component of the order was the student assignment process. It outlined how students would be assigned, allowing for considerable voluntary movement, and what measures would be taken to ensure that at least two-thirds of the schools would be desegregated by September 1977. Again, the only reference to Hispanic students was the permissive paragraph, Section 1 (a) suggested by Gronouski in his February recommendations, which had become Section 3 (j) of the order.

A courtroom packed with Hispanic parents and students observed the presentation of the CWBBAC's attorney, Ness Flores, before Judge Reynolds on the motion to intervene. He argued for an addendum to the court order making section 3 (j) mandatory and pointed out that the student assignment plan could work against Hispanic students if they were still considered under the non-Black classification. The judge took the motion under advisement. The CWBBAC would receive the decision on the motion to intervene on April 13.

During the end of March and first weeks of April, while waiting for the court's decision, the CWBBAC continued to negotiate with the administration regarding proposed expansion of bilingual programs. It appeared more than likely that the board would not object to expansion since it represented more state monies for the district. Bilingual personnel and community representatives had also planned the expansion to enhance desegregation and participation in the process by Hispanic students. Some bilingual centers would be established in schools convenient to Hispanic neighborhoods, thus facilitating transportation. They were also selected in such ways as to modify the feeder pattern of elementary to secondary schools, which had previously resulted in the flow of Hispanic students only to predominantly Hispanic schools, where bilingual programs had been initiated at first. However, the CWBBAC, in negotiating with school personnel, followed the Boston example and insisted on a minimum of three grade levels per bilingual center. Continuation of the developmental and maintenance programs supported in the past by the district was also requested.[76]

The biggest worry of the CWBBAC and Hispanic parents (as expressed before the court on March 25) was the student assignment process as it appeared in the March 17 order. Hispanics and most Milwaukee residents had reservations about how the administration would implement that section of the order since the board's conservative majority would do everything in their power to avoid involuntary assignments of students—specifically Whites. The student assignment process was somewhat complicated and required careful procedures for its implementation to ensure equity in the movement of students. Most parents feared that inadequate procedures and poor informational networks could result in Black and Hispanic children carrying the burden of desegregation.

Court Denies Hispanics' Intervention _____

When the *Denial and Order on Motion to Intervene*[77] was received by the CWBBAC on April 13, the administration interpreted it as meaning that the

Hispanics had to remain within the "non-Black" class and that they had no obligation to respond to Hispanic demands. Hispanics would be treated as White students in the desegregation process. But in fact, the order did more than that. Judge Reynolds recognized in the document that what the CWBBAC sought was to "have the language of paragraph 3 (j) supra, amended so that the paragraph is mandatory rather than permissive."[78] He appeared to have clearly understood that the CWBBAC was not claiming that Milwaukee Public Schools discriminated against Hispanics nor operated segregated schools for Hispanics. He argued that, as it related to "timeliness," it would have been a problem if the CWBBAC had sought a finding of violations of law against the Hispanics. But this was not the case. The CWBBAC desired only to protect the rights of Hispanic students to bilingual education. The denial document supported the *United States* v. *Texas Education Agency* statement and precedent on the rights of third ethnic groups to special consideration during the design of a desegregation remedy. But Reynolds added that

> On the facts of this record, there is no present demonstration of infringement upon the petitioners' interests in bilingual-bicultural programs, nor is there an indication that any harm will devolve on petitioners as a result of remedial actions to be taken.[79]

The document then proceeded to make an important reminder, more to the defendants than to the CWBBAC:

> Moreover, the guidelines described in paragraph 3 (c) of the order (March 17) are a liberalization of the court's prior guidelines in an effort to provide the defendants and the school administration with the flexibility needed to deal fairly with such concerns as bilingual bicultural programs.[80]

Reynolds pointed out that, through the *Statement of Assurances,*

> the defendants have expressed a commitment to continuation of the bilingual bicultural programs. . . . The court has no basis at this time on which to question the defendants' expressed intentions in this area.[81]

But he then reaffirmed the placement of Hispanic students within the "class of non-Black pupils in the main action." However, the administration still could consider paragraph 3 (j) of the March 17 order and the court's recognition of the *Statement of Assurances* a go-ahead signal from the court to treat Hispanics as a separate distinct minority. At least, that is inferred from Reynolds's denial order to which he attached a copy of the *Statement of Assurances.* The document concluded:

> The court is not unmindful of the interests of the petitioners in bilingual-bicultural programs. But as the petitioners have demonstrated no present or likely future impairment of their interests, the motion to intervene will be denied with the understanding that the

petitioners may renew their motion at such time as it appears that their interests are impaired by the remedial course of this school desegregation case.[82]

Again, it appeared, as if based on the *Statement of Assurances*, that Reynolds had faith in Milwaukee Public Schools' commitment to the Hispanic community. What was somewhat contradictory and ironic was how he concluded that the system had defaulted in its obligations to Blacks subsequent to his initial order and continued to resist desegregation, and yet still assumed that they would act in good faith with another minority, the Hispanics.

There was no official response from the administration to the denial of intervention. No statements went to the media on the matter. Internally, administrators proceeded to plan, taking into account existing standards established by the court. The CWBBAC opted for a strategy of getting the administration to stand by its previous commitments. Efforts to comply with the court's most recent order were soon under way, and the office of the bilingual parent coordinator was busy preparing for the student assignment process.

Implementing the "Final" Court Order—1977

During April and May considerable information on the Milwaukee Public Schools' Phase II desegregation plans and on the implementation of the "voluntary approach" plans was disseminated. The administration initiated an aggressive campaign to sell what was to be known as the "choice approach." Under the approach parents would receive a form on which they would list, in order of priority, three or four choices of schools. The administration would attempt to honor the selections but only in ways which would enhance desegregation. The idea was to give parents an opportunity to decide what they wanted for their children rather than to assign students to schools their parents had never heard of. The choice forms had to be in by the end of May; parents who did not participate in the process were warned that their children would be arbitrarily assigned to schools for desegregation purposes. The form enabled parents to choose schools with bilingual programs or to simply indicate that they would prefer a bilingual assignment.

By the end of May Hispanic parents had not been properly informed on what types of bilingual programs were available and at which schools. All that had been released was a form indicating with an asterisk what schools would have bilingual services. This information was inadequate since some schools had kindergarten to grade three programs; others grade four to six, seven to nine, or ten to twelve. In addition, all general information disseminated about the specialty and magnet school programs was released in English, even though the CWBBAC and Hispanic personnel in the administration had been demanding the publication of Spanish materials. The CWBBAC publicly argued that Hispanic parents had no "choice" at all. How could parents choose what they didn't understand?

After the deadline for submission of the choice form had passed, materials translated into Spanish were sent to principals with a hasty memo from the Division of Relationships, that in part read:

> Enclosed is a supply of Info #4's and Info #9's—Spanish version—
> for your use. Quite obviously the arrival of these publications at
> your school is beyond the time of their most effective use. We
> make no apologies. . . .
>
> No distribution method is being recommended. Each principal
> should exercise her/his judgment as to the best use of these
> materials.[83]

Annoyed by the administration's handling of the student assignment
process, the CWBBAC went to the Special Master. Gronouski's negative
reaction to the memo quoted above was loud and prompt. The media
picked up the issue forcing the administration to respond. After a series of
meetings with the CWBBAC, the superintendent assured Hispanic parents
that all Hispanic students wanting bilingual education would receive a
bilingual assignment. The office of the bilingual coordinator was given the
responsibility of bringing to the attention of the assignment units any claims
by Hispanic parents. The problem appeared to have been resolved.

The CWBBAC appreciated the superintendent's willingness to allow any
Hispanic student to participate in bilingual programs in contrast to the practice of other school districts that would provide bilingual services only to
children of limited English ability. Additionally, the superintendent was
proposing that the program be open to non-Hispanic students to ensure that
bilingual classes be, to the extent possible, integrated. It could be inferred
that the superintendent assumed that the Bilingual Education Act of Wisconsin would cover seventy percent of the cost of the total program. Later,
the State Department of Public Instruction announced that it would pay
only for the number of limited English-speaking ability students in the bilingual programs, but this statement did not affect already established plans.

More disappointments were still to come when the administration announced its assignments for September 1977. By mid-June, parents were
receiving their children's assignments and were instructed to visit counseling
centers set up by the administration and run by staff and volunteers. Immediately many Hispanic parents complained to the bilingual parent coordinator and the administration about assignment to schools with no bilingual programs. After assessing the claims, the CWBBAC denounced the
administration for assigning Hispanic children, regardless of whether they
had bilingual needs, to predominantly Black schools with no bilingual programs. It was soon learned that the administration had decided to assign
children of Hispanic parents who had not completed their choice forms to
three predominantly Black schools. All three schools had been rejected by
White parents in making their choices; since the administration considered
Hispanics White for desegregation purposes, they attempted to use them to
desegregate schools other Whites did not want to volunteer to attend.

Under much pressure by the CWBBAC and other prodesegregation
groups throughout the city—including the Committee of 100—the super-

intendent designated the office of the bilingual parent coordinator as a bi-gual counseling/reassignment center. More than 250 Hispanic parents received transfers for their children to schools with bilingual programs. Those Hispanic children whose parents did not request transfers stayed at their newly assigned schools. The CWBBAC estimated that almost 100 Hispanic parents of children assigned to schools they did not choose never requested transfers to schools with bilingual education programs, although the reasons for their actions were not known.

The process of reassignment continued until September. In the inter-vening period one major development in the legal arena confused and angered many Milwaukee parents. On June 28, 1977 the Supreme Court of the United States returned the Milwaukee school desegregation decision to the Seventh Circuit Court of Appeals for reconsideration in view of its decision in the *Dayton*[84] and *Arlington Heights* cases.[85]

The High Court
Calls for Reconsideration

On June 29, 1977, almost one year after the District Court ordered Milwaukee Public Schools to desegregate all of Milwaukee schools, the *Milwaukee Journal* published the text of the Supreme Court's order requiring the Seventh Circuit Court of Appeals to reconsider its affirmation of Judge Reynolds' January 1976 decision and order. In its *per curiam* order the Supreme Court stated:

> Neither the District Court in ordering development of a remedial plan, nor the Court of Appeals in affirming, addressed itself to the inquiry mandated by our opinion...*Dayton Board of Education* v. *Brinkman*, in which we said:
>
>> "If such violations are found, the District Court of Appeals must determine how much incremental segregative effect these violations had on the racial distribution of the Dayton School population, as compared to what it would have been in the absence of such constitutional violations. The remedy must be designed to redress that difference, and only if there has been a systemwide remedy."
>
> The petition for certiorari is accordingly granted, and the judgment of the Court of Appeals is vacated and remanded for reconsideration in the light of *Village of Arlington Heights* v. *Metropolitan Development Corp*...and *Dayton*.[86]

Though attorneys on both sides of the case disagreed on what the order actually meant, most viewed it as a victory for attorney Lawrence Hammond and the board's conservative faction. The latter had consistently argued that Reynolds had overstepped his limits by ordering city-wide desegregation of Milwaukee's schools. On September 1, 1977, the Court of

Appeals vacated (declared void) the Reynolds order and remanded the case to the district court for further proceedings.[87]

The board met immediately to discuss this development and concluded that henceforth they were not obligated to comply with the March 17 order which required the desegregation of all schools by no later than September 1978. Since the student assignment plan was already being implemented, and most students had been assigned for the 1977-1978 school year, they instructed the superintendent to develop a form (ironically called the "White form") which dissatisfied parents could fill out if they wished their children to return to their neighborhood schools. But the Court of Appeals advised the district that the plan agreed upon for September 1977 had to be implemented during the review process and that they were obligated to act in good faith in carrying out its various components.

It had been anticipated that the board's handling of the matter would result in large numbers of parents, especially Whites, requesting changes in their school assignments. However, the short life of the "White form" did not allow for many transfers to occur. When classes began, the number of desegregated schools required by the March order had not been fully met, and there was no legal recourse that the plaintiffs could use to force total compliance. They could only wait for Judge Reynolds to announce when he would reinitiate hearings on the case. It was soon declared that the case would be heard again in its totality on January 3, 1978. Meanwhile the schools already racially balanced continued to function under assigned ratios.

Hammond was to achieve still another victory against prodesegregation forces. He petitioned the Court of Appeals to close the office of the Special Master and his staff. The court, since it had vacated the January 1976 decision, agreed with Hammond. Thus, Gronouski's office disappeared from the scene and with it the invaluable contribution that it had made during the entire desegregation process. The group most affected by the decision was the Desegregation Monitoring Board, a citizens' committee formed by Gronouski to oversee the implementation of Phases II and III of the plan. The Committee of 100 was also in danger. Gronouski's office had always supported their work, and their effectiveness was in part due to his requirement of citizen/community involvement in the desegregation planning. With Gronouski gone, the board, which had been at odds with the group, paid less attention to its recommendations and claims, and the administration considerably reduced its involvement and resource support for its meetings. By late 1977 little was heard of the Committee of 100, and meetings that were usually attended by two to three hundred people were recording an average of twenty-five to fifty persons present.

Impact on Hispanics _____

How was the Hispanic community affected by all the events that followed the Supreme Court's action on the Milwaukee case? Due to the administration's total involvement in the legal battles that ensued, and the fear that the entire voluntary effort would be undone, there was no longer any time for discussion of Hispanic concerns. Consequently, the administration neglected bilingual issues. During the last weeks of August, the CWBBAC charged the Division of Personnel with dragging its feet in assigning bilingual teachers for the September school opening. Qualified bilingual applicants interviewed during the summer months were awaiting positions. But the Division of Personnel refused to assign the new teachers because they were uncertain how an expected court order about treatment of teachers in the desegregation process would define Hispanic and bilingual teachers. Finally they decided, upon reinterpreting the new contract which had resulted from a long and controversial teachers' strike,[88] that bilingual teachers should be assigned to schools as requested by principals based upon their Hispanic populations.

In the interim, many applicants took jobs elsewhere, and during the first week of classes some Black and White monolingual teachers were assigned to bilingual vacancies, resulting in considerable disruption of the bilingual programs and the anger of some Hispanic parents. In other instances, the administration argued that they could not assign bilingual teachers to the already identified and agreed upon bilingual centers because principals had failed to request such personnel in their staff requests for the school year. Some principals complained they had not been properly advised on the procedure to follow. They did not have to request Black teachers and yet they were getting them. Why request bilingual teachers?

Another battle began between the CWBBAC, in alliance with bilingual staff, against the administration. It was soon discovered that of the twenty-four bilingual centers promised for September, only nineteen had received sufficient assignments of Hispanic students to justify bilingual staff. The administration's practice of assigning Hispanic students to predominantly Black schools in June appeared to have had an effect on the number of new bilingual centers contemplated for September 1977. Also, the inadequate information provided to Hispanic parents prior to the submission of their choice forms probably limited the number of parents knowledgeable about the proposed bilingual centers.

Schools with existing bilingual programs from previous years continued to offer the same or, in many cases, expanded services. The number of Hispanic students in bilingual programs had increased significantly.[89] Bilingual staff increased also, in spite of the neglect of the Division of Personnel.[90]

The status of Hispanic bilingual teachers during faculty desegregation remains unclear. Approval of state standards for the certification of bilingual teachers may help to clarify the status of teachers in the bilingual programs. However, in Milwaukee there will be no guarantee that bilingual teachers will be assigned to bilingual classes unless new contractual language is added or interpreted to the advantage of the program.[91]

In October 1977 the bilingual parent coordinator resigned. In his letter of resignation he warned the administration that by failing to give official identifiable standing to Hispanic students and staff in the desegregation process they were setting the grounds for violation of equal opportunity rights. He also made specific recommendations to the superintendent regarding ways to facilitate equal treatment and benefits for Hispanic students. His most important recommendation was one suggested many times by the CWBBAC but always ignored: the establishment of a Bilingual Department within the Milwaukee Public Schools' organizational and administrative structure, similar in status to the Department of Exceptional Education.

The impact of his resignation had little effect on the continued involvement of Hispanic parents with the school system. Some changes had taken place, however. Although involvement by large masses of parents and community persons was less visible, the coordinator's efforts had resulted in the formation of a highly effective and sophisticated cadre of parents who participated in citizen organizations and school committees throughout the city.

The constant demand for expansion of bilingual programs by both Hispanic and non-Hispanic groups led Superintendent McMurrin to announce that maintenance and developmental programs would continue and would be open to any child. McMurrin also indicated interest in developing a Spanish-language-proficiency magnet school for 1978-1979 which would include both Hispanic and non-Hispanic children, but this was not recommended by the administration.

An Out-of-Court Settlement—1979

By 1978 it was evident that both community leadership and the schools were tired of desegregation litigation. The court held evidentiary hearings during January and February, 1978, trying to establish, again, whether there had been intentional segregation by the school system. On June 1, 1978, the court issued another decision finding that Milwaukee school officials had administered the system with intent to segregate Black children since 1950. More legal maneuvering followed. On February 8, 1979, the court re-affirmed that the effects of the school officials' actions were system-wide and that a city-wide desegregation plan was required. On March 1, 1979, a settlement agreement was submitted to the court. The settlement notice indicated that the majority of board members believed that a continuation of litigation would be "distracting" and that the children would be best served by "the establishment of a spirit of trust and cooperation" (see Appendix B).

The School Board appealed the February 8, 1979 order, and the plaintiffs were worried that the Supreme Court would again vacate and force another trial. Pending litigation before the high court (the *Dayton* and *Columbus* cases as well as the court's decision on the *Bakke* case)[92] suggested that it was possible Reynolds's decision could be reversed. Thus, the attorneys for the plaintiffs called for an out-of-court agreement.

The agreement was accepted by the School Board in a split vote (9-6), with all Black board members and some conservatives opposing the agreement, and most conservatives and some liberals voting in the affirmative. Opposition from the conservatives centered on their adamant refusal to admit to any purposeful segregation, while Blacks opposed the agreement because it allowed some schools to remain 100 percent Black. The members voting to approve the settlement voiced a desire to end the long litigation and to get on with the job of improving the school system.[93]

Community response to the proposals contained in the settlement was mostly negative. The local media highlighted negative reactions and, in an unusual move, Judge Reynolds announced that he would hear directly from

Milwaukeeans regarding the settlement. He called for two days of hearings during which those opposing the settlement could speak and present written statements or evidence substantiating their claims. Fifty-six of the individuals and community-based organizations submitting written requests to appear before the court were allowed to do so. On March 26 and 27, 1979, they each made ten-minute presentations that clearly covered all ideological and political extremes in the community. A substantial number of Blacks testified against the settlement, including the School Board's Black members.

The CWBBAC also made an appearance before the court in opposition to the settlement. Its main objections related not only to the desegregation case itself but also to events which had been occurring since mid-1978.

The Office for Civil Rights Intervention _____

Since September 1978, the Hispanic community had been monitoring the investigation which the HEW Office for Civil Rights initiated as a result of a complaint filed three years earlier by the Latin Council of Wisconsin, a statewide advocacy group formed in 1972 to improve conditions for Hispanics in Wisconsin. The purpose of the OCR review of the Milwaukee Public Schools was to determine the system's status related to compliance with Title VI of the Civil Rights Act. More specifically, OCR wanted to determine whether Milwaukee schools had adequately provided for the language needs of its national origin student population. It had been a difficult task for OCR officials because Superintendent McMurrin was reluctant to comply with OCR's request for information on services provided to national origin minority students. McMurrin repeatedly claimed that there were no violations against Hispanics or any other language minority, that they were being adequately served, and that Milwaukee had the best bilingual program in the country. An angry Hispanic community confronted him because they felt that his position, which appeared somewhat arrogant, was inconsistent with the facts as they knew them.

In a letter to the district in December, 1978, OCR corroborated the claims brought forth by Hispanics. OCR charged that Milwaukee schools had violated the rights of Hispanics and other language minorities in that:

1. The district failed to adequately identify and assess non- and limited-English-speaking national origin minority students.

2. The district failed to take adequate affirmative steps to ensure that non- and limited-English-speaking children received equally effective educational services.

3. The district failed to adequately identify, assess, and provide services to non- and limited-English-speaking national origin minority group children in need of exceptional education instruction.

4. The district did not provide all parents of non- and limited-English-speaking national origin minority students with regular school notices in their primary language.

In the same letter OCR charged that existing bilingual programs were only of the Spanish/English type and that the district had ignored the needs of approximately 400 students from other language groups. The letter called for a comprehensive educational plan to correct the violations found and advised the district that failure to comply could endanger its ESAA (Emergency School Aid Act) grants as well as other federal funding.

Again McMurrin refused to accept OCR's findings and by mid-January, 1979, little had been done to comply. Hispanics, annoyed by McMurrin's handling of the matter, went to Black community members and local organizations and charged that McMurrin was endangering federal desegregation monies with his refusal to respond to OCR's request for a plan. Media coverage of the situation forced the superintendent to agree to negotiations. However, his staff announced that all dealings and agreements with OCR would be kept strictly between the administration and OCR. Surprised board members would later read in local newspapers of OCR's charges; even they had been kept in the dark by the superintendent. An agreement with OCR was in the works when the desegregation court rendered its February 8, 1979 decision.

Hispanics Debate the Settlement

Judge Reynolds's decision to hold a hearing was seen by many Hispanics as another opportunity to highlight their concerns. However, the proposed settlement made some provisions for the treatment of Hispanic students that sparked considerable debate within the Hispanic community. A series of meetings were held between the CWBBAC and other concerned Hispanic educators. The controversy centered upon two factors: (1) the proposal to exempt four predominantly Hispanic schools—all of which had extensive bilingual programs—from the desegregation process; and (2) the provision that all schools with combined minority populations in which bilingual programs existed or would be established had to have at least 12.5 percent Black students and no less than 12.5 percent of the other minority (evidently Hispanics). Supporters of the settlement felt that it protected bilingual education programming while opponents argued that the settlement made no provisions to protect the proposed exempted schools from becoming segregated minority buildings. It was also feared that demographic changes in the Hispanic community could lead to the use of Hispanic students as Whites for future desegregation purposes. Furthermore, opponents claimed that the settlement ignored the concurrent OCR compliance agreement and did not include provisions for the treatment of Hispanic staff.

The Hispanic leaders decided to make a presentation at the March hearing which would oppose the settlement. Milwaukee Hispanics wanted the record to reflect their support for Blacks seeking desegregation and their desire to be included in all desegregation developments. A statement was prepared and delivered to the court on March 26, 1979.[94]

In May, 1979, the court approved the out-of-court settlement and issued an order that incorporated all of its contents. Opposition from the Black community was considerable, and immediately after the settlement was approved, the local NAACP, supported by the organization's national office and legal counsel, filed an appeal with the Seventh Circuit Court of Appeals.

Also in May, 1979, the school district announced that an agreement had been reached with OCR on the Title VI violations. Critics of the agreement argued that the district refused to allow Hispanic community involvement. Even Hispanic personnel working for the district—including members of the central office bilingual staff—were kept from having any significant input in the negotiated document. Nonetheless, the superintendent submitted it to the School Board and almost a quarter of a million dollars from local funds were approved to cover the cost of program expansions promised for the 1979-1980 school year.

Hispanics continue to seek involvement in the desegregation case and expansion of bilingual services will occur in 1979-1980. However, the relationship between the administration and the Hispanic community is not one of trust and cooperation. A return to confrontation strategies remains possible. Community leaders will continue to monitor the implementation of bilingual education and race desegregation for years to come.

Conclusions

This monograph focused on the political decision-making processes involved in one city's experience in implementing school desegregation as seen from the point of view of a Hispanic community's efforts to influence the decision makers. Such descriptive efforts are all but nonexistent in the literature on desegregation and bilingual education as well.[95] Aside from court decisions themselves, we lack an adequate understanding of how Hispanics go about trying to get their views heard before and after a ruling is made, even if they are not intervenors in the case; how Blacks, engaged in the long and tiresome battles for desegregation, react when faced with attempts to include Hispanic concerns in shaping desegregation remedies; how school boards deal with attempts by community members to gain assurances that the legitimate educational needs of linguistic minorities will figure prominently in their plans; and how administrators cope when faced with implementing complex educational change in a context of general community mobilization, and perhaps polarization, brought about by court-ordered desegregation and demands for educational equity by Hispanics.

One city's experience is just that: a political and social context, a series of events, a set of actors and their interactions. It cannot be assumed that the situation is exactly comparable to the experiences of other cities; in the absence of other descriptive studies and comparative analyses, readers will have to make their own judgments. The particular legal realities in this case, the numbers of Hispanic students involved (six percent of the school population), the stage of implementation of bilingual education within the district at the time of the court ruling, the existence of state bilingual legislation, the openness of the planning process, the high degree of involvement by parent/citizen groups throughout the process, the role of the media, and the organizing skills of the participants—all of these factors and others must be considered.

It is important to recognize that the Hispanic community in Milwaukee was not trying to prevent or delay the desegregation ruling or to inappropriately impede the planning process. The attempt to intervene in the court case was made due to the fear that the administration, the lawyers for the plaintiffs, and the board would destroy or severely impair existing bilingual programs which had been developing over several years. While the district had shown commitment to educational change for Hispanics by applying for federal funds and by adding local money for these programs, the current desegregation issue was conceived of in Black-White terms only. Therefore, there was real reason to have a lack of trust in how the administration planners and the school board would act under increasing community pressure from other self-interest groups.

Of course, this situation is not unique to Milwaukee. Hispanic groups in other communities, busy implementing new programs won after much effort, have had to face a new political and legal crisis in which they are not even recognized as legitimate participants. The timing of their interventions often makes them appear to be against any integration. However, this is not true for the most part. The objections center primarily on being ignored in a Black-White battle. The decision makers often wish to maintain the maximum flexibility and may ignore Hispanic demands or use them as an excuse to resist desegregation. In the eyes of some administrators, desegregation seems possible without placing a burden on Whites if Hispanic children are defined as White and bused to Black schools. Others, posing an irreconcilable conflict between bilingual education and desegregation, may try to pit Blacks and Hispanics against one another to prevent change.

The issue of legal definition as an "identifiable minority" emerged in Milwaukee, as it has in other cities. In some desegregation cases judges have ruled that Hispanic children are an identifiable minority and must be included in any remedy planned by a district. (See *Cisneros* v. *Corpus Christi*,[96] *Keyes*,[97] and *U.S.* v. *Texas Education Agency*[98].) In other cases, as in Milwaukee, the rulings did not make this distinction, and Hispanic intervention in the court case was denied. In Milwaukee school authorities have tried to maintain flexibility, even attempting at one point to categorize Hispanic children in bilingual programs as minority and those not in programs as White. This obviously was not acceptable to the Hispanic parent group. The court maintained Hispanics were non-Black, providing flexibility to meet their needs through different quotas. On the other hand, the state defined them as minority by legislative action in Chapter 220. Because this identification issue was not resolved by the court, it was imperative that other avenues be used to clarify the status of Hispanic children. This involved a multifocused strategy and continuous monitoring of the planning and implementation process by Hispanic parents.

Open Planning Process, but Negotiation behind the Scenes

The openness of the planning process for desegregation provides the possibility for some equalization of power for minority groups normally not part of the decision-making process. There is a legitimate channel for them to bring their concerns to the attention of the community. The broad-based structure that had developed in Milwaukee allowed for conflicts to surface; at the same time, participants maintained a task orientation that fostered conflict resolution and collaboration. Existing community groups in favor of voluntary desegregation could be more active in forging a community consensus. Hispanic parents representing their neighborhoods could voice their concerns and develop allies. The administration could continue to foster collaboration and function as a manager of the process as well as use the process to sell its own ideas to the public.

The Hispanic community in Milwaukee took advantage of this open planning process and was successful in making the court and the district more attentive to their concerns. They were also able through their participation to develop relationships with other parents and community representatives. The plan prepared by the Committee of 100 and the administration reflected this collaboration. However, it is clear that most of the key decisions were negotiated by lawyers and administrators with limited involvement of community members.

Multiple Strategies_____

Being numerically small and not an affected group in the eyes of the court, Hispanic parents could not limit their influence efforts to the Committee of 100. It was unclear whether the board, the Special Master, and the superintendent would endorse all the proposals developed by the Committee of 100. Therefore, direct efforts to influence these important decision makers were undertaken: the board was asked to approve a policy protecting Hispanic programs and ensure community input in the process through the *Statement of Assurances;* links to liberal board members were established; the administration's implementation efforts were continually monitored, thereby enabling the community to react to potential and real injustices. When inequality was involved, such as in the failure to provide timely information in Spanish about the bilingual centers, the magnet programs, and the student assignment process, Hispanic parents fought to modify these procedures so that their particular concerns would be taken into account. The Special Master, a key figure in the whole process, was continually kept informed through formal as well as informal channels; and many meetings were held with him or his assistant. The success of these meetings was reflected in his reports to the judge in which he included comments and suggestions regarding the importance of considering the educational needs of Hispanic and other minority children in the development and implementation of desegregation plans.

Prior existence of well-developed bilingual programs was important in protecting Hispanic parents' concerns. The School Board had already accepted the legitimate need for these programs, and no struggle was required to justify their value. A sizeable staff existed and local monetary commitments had already been made, and it was unlikely that the desegregation process would reverse all previous gains. In addition, Hispanic educators within the school system had access to information about administration plans. In order to have continuous access to information and, therefore, some possibility of maintaining control over the flow of events, it was most useful to have people inside the school system who not only were informed about the plans of the educational bureaucracy at various levels, but also had a legitimate way to influence key decision makers.

A well-organized and dedicated core group of parents was a legitimate community voice speaking to the school district. However, survival of an effective parent/community group over time is difficult. Committed and informed help is always needed. In Milwaukee the parent coordinator was able to serve this function.

The fact that Wisconsin had a state law requiring bilingual programming and providing for costs incurred by school districts was also of great importance in expanding existing bilingual programs. Often desegregation monopolizes the resources of a district, and it is extremely helpful to have state or federal support for establishing and expanding bilingual programs.

The Media

The media is a useful tool to bring issues to public attention and hold decision makers accountable. In Milwaukee the Hispanic parents were able to win the attention of the media, and they kept in constant touch with TV stations and the press, thus ensuring appropriate coverage. Since they were without direct decision-making authority in terms of the court, the board, or the administration, they needed to try to influence community opinion makers and decision makers through the media.

Implications for the Future

Hispanic parents in Milwaukee were prepared for continuous monitoring of the desegregation process. Hard work and the willingness to attend numerous meetings at all hours and to draft statements and proposals were essential to whatever measure of success the CWBBAC attained. While intervention in the case was unsuccessful, the fact that legal action was taken indicated to all decision makers the strength of Hispanic concern. Help was accepted from White and Black local allies and desegregation experts, both local and national. Information was available about what was happening elsewhere in the country regarding a changing legal scene. Multiple strategies were used, and some quick learning about desegregation took place. Hispanic parents were successful for the most part in bringing attention to the issues. This vigilance on the part of Hispanic parents in Milwaukee needs to continue. Educational and legal decisions will continue to be made in a political context in which parents must remain visible and active.

Nationally, there is a need for the Hispanic community to make its concerns heard so that judges, planners, and administrators at the local level will not be able to ignore issues affecting Hispanics. It must be made clear that when cities are multiethnic and multilingual, planning for desegregation must include all children's needs at every stage. One attempt to clarify the issues and gain national perspective took place a few years ago. In June 1977 the National Institute of Education sponsored a conference "Desegregation and Education Concerns of the Hispanic Community" involving parents, lawyers, educators, and researchers. (A report of the proceedings is available.⁹⁹) Follow-up activities are needed which will enable social scientists and community members to jointly examine the political decision-making processes over time, in depth, and with a comparative perspective. Also needed are descriptive studies of program models that seem to be effective in producing social and cognitive benefits to Black, Hispanic, White, and other children learning through integrated quality education.

The long-range goals of bilingual education and desegregation need not conflict, although in specific cities the implementation of these two mandates may well result in conflict. The legal issues are still evolving along with implementation strategies which are educationally sound for all children affected. Decisions will continue to be influenced by a variety of factors: changing interpretations of law by judges; legislative mandates and their implementation; federal regulations, compliance activities, and financial incentives; expert witnesses and court-appointed masters; the media; financial exigencies; and pressures from various community groups.

For Hispanics, who traditionally have been excluded from decision-making processes, desegregation will continue to involve battles for recognition and meaningful participation. It is possible that what happened in Milwaukee will bring additional attention to the difficulties Hispanics are having in getting decision makers to respond to their legitimate concerns about providing equality of educational opportunity. The legal, political, and educational issues faced in Milwaukee may find themselves, sooner or later, part of the process of educational conflict and change in all multiethnic cities in America.

Appendixes

Appendix A

Major Issues, Assurances, and Legal Principles Affecting the Hispanic Pupil During Desegregation Efforts

Prepared by the City-Wide Bilingual Bicultural Advisory Committee (CWBBAC) and approved by the Milwaukee School Board, October 5, 1976.

The need and importance of bilingual bicultural education in a systematic and continuous developmental program in the Milwaukee Public Schools for children of limited English ability and for maximizing other children's language potential and cultural understanding and appreciation has been recognized and endorsed by official action of the Board of School Directors. Pertinent federal legislation and the Bilingual Bicultural Legislation Act (Chapter 395, Wisconsin Laws, 1975) support and require bilingual bicultural education as a viable approach for providing equal educational opportunities for limited English ability students. There are also judicial and legal precedents that have found violations of the Civil Rights Act, Title VI, when bilingual bicultural programs are nonexistent or nonavailable to pupils in need of them (*Serna* v. *Portales; Lau* v. *Nichols*).

Bilingual bicultural education and integration are compatible and feasible. Both efforts are attempts at providing equality of educational opportunity for pupils. Bilingual bicultural education programs are to enhance integration efforts as opposed to having a segregative effect. Social and cultural interaction are further assets to language and cultural maintenance.

The Milwaukee Public Schools' bilingual bicultural program is at present in the Spanish-English area. It mainly serves pupils of Hispanic descent enrolled in the Milwaukee Public Schools but is available to any child.

In order to assure continuity of bilingual bicultural education programming and equal educational opportunities for Hispanic pupils and for other ethnic/language groups as might appear necessary during desegregation efforts, the Board of School Directors needs to endorse and commit itself to the following:

1. Hispanic pupils need to be considered an ethnic/racial/minority group, and an identifiable class, forming part of the "minority group pupil" population of the Milwaukee Public School System.

2. The combined numbers of "minority group pupils" shall be kept within the ratios set by the court order.

3. Schools with Hispanic pupil enrollment constituting most or all of the minority pupil population shall be considered desegregated if the percentages of minority pupils fall within those set by the court.

4. Criteria shall be set, in accordance with Chapter 395, to determine bilingual bicultural needs and eligibility to bilingual bicultural programs of Hispanic pupils volunteering for specialty programs. Parents of pupils eligible for bilingual bicultural education programming shall so be advised prior to the honoring of any transfer request to a nonbilingual specialty program.

5. The transportation of Hispanic pupils to other schools, different from those they are in attendance at, shall take place in accordance with the Pupil Transfer Policy and the Board-adopted Transportation Policy.

6. Hispanic pupils' right to bilingual bicultural education programming will always be observed in line with the principles of equality of educational opportunity and guided by the rules set forth by the Bilingual Bicultural Education Act, Chapter 395, Laws of Wisconsin, 1975. This also shall apply to other ethnic/language groups participating in bilingual bicultural education programs.

7. The special status of teachers in bilingual bicultural education programs with regard to seniority is recognized. Teachers needed in bilingual bicultural education programs will be assigned and/or retained in schools in response to bilingual bicultural education needs.

   The categorization and implications of the movement/transfer of Hispanic and bilingual teachers as per the court order shall be discussed, negotiated, and resolved with the bargaining units, and the final agreements will become part of this statement of assurances.

8. The Board shall adopt the above as part of the planning for phase two and three of the desegregation/integration plan.

Appendix B

Notice to Class Members
of the Proposed Settlement of
the Milwaukee Public School Desegregation Case
and of the Hearing on that Settlement

TO: All students presently enrolled or who will enroll in the Milwaukee public school system, their parents and their guardians:

You are hereby notified pursuant to Rule 23(e) of the Federal Rules of Civil Procedure that a hearing will be held on March 26, 1979, at 9:30 A.M. before the Honorable John W. Reynolds, Chief Judge of the United States District Court for the Eastern District of Wisconsin, at the United States Courthouse, 517 East Wisconsin Avenue, Milwaukee, Wisconsin, in his Courtroom, Room 425, pursuant to an order of the Court dated March 6, 1979.

The purpose of the hearing is to determine whether a proposed settlement of this action, commonly known as the Milwaukee Public School Desegregation Case, should be approved by this Court as fair, reasonable and adequate. If the settlement is approved by the Court, the members of the plaintiff classes, including yourself, will be bound by the settlement, subject to the right of appeal.

At a hearing on March 5, 1979, the Court found that the settlement proposal is within the range of possible approval and that there is probable cause to submit it to members of the class and to hold a hearing on its fairness at which all interested parties will have an opportunity to be heard. The Court also found that this notice is fair and adequate.

History of this Case

This action was commenced in 1965 as a class action on behalf of all present and future school children in the Milwaukee Public School system. A 30-

day trial was held in 1973 and 1974, and on January 19, 1976, the Court rendered a decision finding that the Milwaukee Public School System was unconstitutionally segregated and ordering that a desegregation plan be developed. Shortly following this decision, the Milwaukee Teachers' Education Association ("MTEA") was allowed to intervene as a party and participate in matters relating to remedy insofar as they affect teachers. On March 17, 1977, the Court approved a final desegregation plan and ordered the defendants to implement that plan through December 31, 1980.

The defendants took separate appeals of the Court's January 19, 1976 and March 17, 1977 orders. The United States Court of Appeals for the Seventh Circuit affirmed the January 19, 1977 order, but the United States Supreme Court, on January 29, 1977, vacated the decision of the Court of Appeals and remanded the case to the Court of Appeals for reconsideration in light of two intervening Supreme Court decisions. On September 1, 1977, the Court of Appeals vacated this Court's January 19, 1976 and March 17, 1977 orders and remanded the case to this Court for further proceedings on the issues of whether or not the defendants had administered the Milwaukee Public School System with an intent to segregate and what present effects, if any, resulted from any intentionally segregative conduct found by the Court. The Court of Appeals and this Court ordered that a portion of the desegregation plan contained in this Court's March 17, 1977 order stay in effect for the 1977-78 school year.

The court held an evidentiary hearing during January and February, 1978, on the issue of whether or not the defendants had engaged in intentional segregation. On June 1, 1978, the Court issued a decision finding that the defendants had administered the school system with segregative intent at least since 1950 and in doing so violated the rights of the plaintiffs under the United States Constitution.

On August 2, 1978, as a consequence of a request by defendants for additional time to prepare for the hearings on present effects, the Court ordered that an interim desegregation plan be implemented during the 1978-79 school year.

In July and October, 1978, the Court held an evidentiary hearing on the issue of what present effects resulted from the intentionally segregative acts found by the Court. On February 8, 1979, the Court issued a decision holding that the present effects were systemwide and directed the parties to submit proposed desegregation plans designed to remedy those present effects.

On March 1, 1979, in lieu of separate submissions of desegregation plans by the plaintiffs and defendants, a Settlement Agreement dealing with all issues other than the teacher desegregation remedy was submitted to the Court. It is this Settlement Agreement which prompted this notice to class members.

Reasons for Settlement of this Class Action _____

Plaintiffs and some members of the Board of School Directors of the City of Milwaukee ("Board") believe that the Court's June 1, 1978 and February 8, 1979 Decisions are valid. Some members of the Board disagree and believe that (1) there were no actions engaged in by the Board which were taken with the intent to discriminate, (2) there were no present effects even if the violation findings were to withstand appellate scrutiny, (3) the legal premises applied by the Court are invalid and (4) these decisions would be reversed if appealed to higher courts. Nevertheless, the respective parties to this Agreement believe that settlement of this class action is desirable because (1) a majority of the Board believes that a continuation of the litigation would be distracting and the Board's primary attention should be focused upon educational concerns, (2) defendants have already implemented over two and one-half years of a court-ordered desegregation program, (3) the Board advocates a desegregation program which is primarily premised upon principles of voluntarism and concepts previously developed and announced by the Board in its (a) Statement on Education and Human Rights and (b) Options for Learning and Schools for the Transition announcements and (4) plaintiffs and the majority of the Board recognize that settlement will terminate this action, without adversary hearings on remedy and further appeals. It is believed that the best interests of the parties and the children attending the Milwaukee Public Schools will be served by the termination of this litigation and by the establishment of a spirit of trust and cooperation.

Terms of the Settlement Agreement _____

The Settlement Agreement negotiated by the plaintiffs and defendants provides for the entry of an order by the Court covering all aspects of this action except those relating to the desegregation of faculties. The faculty desegregation remedy will be determined by the Court. The Agreement further provides that no appeals will be taken by the parties to the Agreement (although parties who appear and object to the Agreement in the manner set forth below will retain their right to appeal in the event the Court approves the Agreement). A summary of the operative terms of the order is attached as an Exhibit to this notice. This order will, if approved by the Court and if you do not appear and object to the Agreement in the manner set forth below, be your sole remedy for the constitutional violations found in this Court's previous decisions and orders. Please study the exhibit carefully. It may affect your rights.

Faculty Desegregation Goals _____

The plaintiffs and defendants have jointly submitted a plan for faculty desegregation which differs from that submitted by the MTEA. All parties, including the MTEA, are in substantial agreement that any plan which might be approved by the Court would have at least the following as goals for the desegregation of faculties:

A. Definition of a desegregated faculty for fall, 1979:

1. At least two-thirds (2/3) of the schools would meet the goal of desegregating the faculties when the faculties in those schools are within a plus (+) or minus (-) five (5) percentage points of the percentage that the total number of black teachers is to the total number of teachers within the school system.

2. At least one-sixth (1/6) of the schools would meet the goal of desegregating the faculties when the faculties in those schools are within a plus (+) or minus (-) ten (10) percentage points of the percentage that the total number of black teachers is to the total number of teachers within the school system.

B. Definition of a desegregated faculty for fall, 1980, 1981, 1982, 1983:

1. At least two-thirds (2/3) of the schools would meet the goal of desegregating the faculties when the faculties in those schools are within a plus (+) or minus (-) five (5) percentage points of the percentage that the total number of black teachers is to the total number of teachers within the school system.

2. At least one-third (1/3) of the schools would meet the goal of desegregating the faculties when the faculties in those schools are within a plus (+) or minus (-) ten (10) percentage points of the percentage that the total number of black teachers is to the total number of teachers within the school sytem.

The Hearing

At the hearing at 9:30 A.M. on March 26, 1979, in Room 425 of the Federal Building, 517 East Wisconsin Avenue, Milwaukee, Wisconsin, you may appear in person or by counsel and make an oral presentation setting forth why the proposed settlement either should or should not be approved by the Court as fair, reasonable and adequate. If you or your counsel wish to make an oral presentation at the hearing, you must, on or before March 22, 1979, file with the Clerk of this Court a written notice stating your intention to appear and stating the position you will advocate before the Court. As an alternative to making an oral presentation, you or your counsel may file with the Clerk of Court on or before March 22, 1979, a written statement setting forth why the proposed settlement either should or should not be approved by the Court as fair, reasonable and adequate. The written notice or any written statement must be taken to or mailed to:

Clerk of the Court
United States District Court
Eastern District of Wisconsin
Room 362 Federal Building
517 East Wisconsin Avenue
Milwaukee, Wisconsin 53202

Do not write or call Judge Reynolds directly.

If you are satisfied with the settlement, you need do nothing. If you are not satisfied with it, you should follow the procedure set forth above.

If the Settlement Agreement is not approved by the Court, you will be bound by the outcome of future litigation in this case, regardless of whether that outcome is favorable or adverse to you.

Examination of Pleadings and Papers _____

The foregoing references to the pleadings and orders in this case, as well as the terms of the Settlement Agreement as summarized in the Exhibit, are only summaries. The complete texts are on file with the Clerk of the Court, United States District Court for the Eastern District of Wisconsin, 517 East Wisconsin Avenue, Milwaukee, Wisconsin 53202, under the file number set forth above and are available for inspection there.

Dated March 6, 1979, at Milwaukee, Wisconsin.

UNITED STATES DISTRICT COURT
EASTERN DISTRICT OF WISCONSIN

By: /s/ Ruth W. LaFave

Ruth W. LaFave
Clerk of the Court

Exhibit to Notice to Class Members
of the Proposed Settlement of
the Milwaukee Public School Desegregation Case

The following is a summary of the operative terms of an order which may be entered by the Court if it approves the Settlement Agreement negotiated by the parties.

I. Injunctive Provisions

The Settlement Agreement contains an injunction which runs against the Board, its members, the Superintendent, the Secretary-Business Manager and all successors and agents. It prohibits discrimination upon the basis of race in the operation of the schools with respect to any matter which was the subject of the litigation.

II. Student Desegregation

Any student desiring to attend a "desegregated" school shall have the right to do so, and defendants shall annually advise all students in writing of this right. A desegregated school for purposes of student desegregation is defined as:

1. Each elementary or junior high school which has a student population composed of not less than 25% and not more than 60% black students and

2. Each senior high school which has a student population composed of not less than 20% and not more than 60% black students.

While the order is pending, defendants shall assign students in good faith with the goal of having at least the following number of students enrolled in schools within the Milwaukee Public School System which are desegregated:

1. When the system percentage of blacks is 50% or less, three-fourths of the "base number" of students or

2. When the system percentage of blacks is more than 50%, three-fourths of the "base number" of students times a fraction consisting of the number of non-black students over the number of black students.

The "base number" used to compute the number of students to be in desegregated schools is all students in the system except:

1. Kindergarten and pre-kindergarten students,

2. Exceptional education students attending schools devoted exclusively to exceptional education, and

3. Those students enrolled in Vieau, Allen-Field, Kagel and Kosciuszko, as long as these schools have a bilingual education program.

In addition, each elementary and junior high school (except those listed above) will have either:

1. A minimum black student enrollment of 25% or

2. Where the school has a bilingual education program, a minimum combined minority enrollment of 25% with at least 12.5% black students and at least 12.5% other minority students.

Additionally, all senior high schools which are not otherwise desegregated will have a minimum of 250 black students.

Nothing in the order prevents defendants from having more students attending desegregated schools than the number specified in the order.

The student transfer policies and programs now in effect will continue. These require that transfers contribute to the racial balance in the school to which the student seeks to transfer.

Finally, defendants will be ordered to develop and implement a human relations program for students, the objectives of which shall be to aid the achievement of quality education and successful desegregation and integration, and the details of which shall be within the sole discretion of defendants. This program shall be implemented in each school year during which the order remains in effect.

III. Desegregation Monitoring

Overall responsibility for monitoring compliance with the Court order which will be entered if the proposal is approved by the Court is vested in United States Magistrate John C. McBride. In addition, a five-member panel designated the "monitoring board" will have jurisdiction to review complaints filed by members of the plaintiff classes regarding whether or not the order is being complied with. Members of the monitoring board are to be selected by mutual agreement of the parties and shall serve as volunteers, without compensation.

Complaints must be initiated by the affected class member or members who have direct knowledge of the veracity of the complaint and who have been adversely affected. Assistance in the complaint procedure may be provided by a parent, legal guardian, attorney or community group.

The monitoring board shall have the right to visit schools and to obtain information from defendants which will enable the monitoring board to make a determination relative to any properly filed complaint or to permit it to perform its duties.

Once a complaint is received, defendants have the first opportunity to respond to it, but in the event this response is unsatisfactory to the monitoring board, it may resolve the matter. If either party is dissatisfied with the monitoring board's decision, an appeal may be taken to the Magistrate, and eventually to the Court if requested.

Secretarial services and reimbursement for reasonable expenses are to be provided to the monitoring board by defendants.

In addition, the monitoring procedure specifies certain reporting requirements with respect to the desegregation goals which have been established and provides a mechanism for information and documents to be obtained by counsel for the plaintiffs if necessary.

IV. School Openings and Closings and the Locations of Specialty Programs

Future decisions by defendants with respect to school openings, school closings and the locations of specialty school programs will not be determined in a racially discriminatory manner.

V. Duration

The Settlement Agreement specifies that the desegregation program shall remain in effect for five years. On July 1, 1984, if the requirements of the order have been complied with, the order lapses and is of no further force and effect and the action will then be dismissed with prejudice.

VI. Fees and Costs

The Settlement Agreement provides for a payment to Irvin B. Charne, counsel for the absent members of the plaintiff classes, of $329,350.00, and to Lloyd A. Barbee, counsel for the named plaintiffs, of $563,428.11. These payments would cover all fees, costs and expenses through the date of the signing of the order. Mr. Charne's fees are to be paid before May 31, 1979, and Mr. Barbee's fees will be paid through an initial payment of $113,428.11 before May 31, 1979, and payments of $90,000.00 per year for five additional years.

VII. Dismissal of Counsel for Unnamed Plaintiffs_____

The Settlement Agreement provides that Mr. Charne is relieved from his appointment as counsel except with respect to those matters relating to the determination of a remedy for faculty desegregation. To the extent Mr. Charne is relieved from his appointment, Mr. Barbee is to represent the plaintiff classes.

VIII. Final Order _____

The order to be entered is a final order directing the defendants to implement a plan for the desegregation of the Milwaukee Public School System. The Court will issue the order with an awareness of the requirements set forth in the Emergency School Aid Act for receiving federal aids.

Appendix C

Statement on Behalf of the City-Wide Bilingual Bicultural Advisory Committee and Other Concerned Hispanic Citizens

Presented before the Honorable John W. Reynolds at the March 26, 1979 hearing regarding a proposed settlement of the Milwaukee desegregation case, *Armstrong et al.* v. *O'Connell et al.*

Your Honor:

Again Hispanics appear before this Court to voice concerns and objections to another proposed remedy in this lengthy litigation. Some of the remarks that will follow later are not new to this Court. Most were voiced during the spring of 1977 when the City-Wide Bilingual Bicultural Advisory Committee (CWBBAC) sought to intervene in the case to protect the rights of Hispanic students during the framing of what was to become the final order of desegregation. This Court is aware of its denial of intervention as well as its promise to allow Hispanics to again approach the Court should there appear to be an imminent danger to the existing and contemplated bilingual education programs. Although this is not a motion to intervene, we feel that certain deleterious effects can result from the definitions, language, and/or absence of language in the proposed settlement regarding the treatment of all Hispanic students in the Milwaukee Public Schools (MPS) system, on Hispanic and bilingual personnel, and on the continuation and expansion of bilingual services.

Before going into the specific concerns we bring today, we find it necessary to go on record as being unequivocally in support of the right of Black children and all children to an equal educational opportunity and equal benefits from the schooling experience which, in multiethnic and multilingual urban communities, cannot truly exist in a segregated environment. We support the efforts and gains of Black parents in their quest to eradicate racial isolation and discriminatory practices by schools and other institutions in America. We are further concerned with the fact that the proposed settlement will not desegregate all schools. However, we do understand that settling the matter out of court, within reasonable parameters and assurances to plaintiffs, may be the most expeditious and, perhaps, in the final analysis, the way to allow for the most comprehensive desegregation implementation possible under present circumstances. But we urge the Court to ensure provisions in the final settlement that will at a minimum guarantee Milwaukee parents direct involvement through structures set up and supported for such purposes.

Our statement is premised on four propositions:

1. that Hispanic and other national origin minority group students in MPS are legally entitled to programs that promote equality of educational opportunity;

2. that bilingual bicultural education is an effective means of promoting this goal;

3. that no remedy (or, in this instance, proposed settlement) in a desegregation case can be effective if it is detrimental to other non-Black minorities; and

4. that no remedy can ignore the changing demographic picture in Milwaukee where Hispanics live within identifiable residential boundaries, and continue to grow both in absolute numbers as well as in proportion to other students in the schools, given the reality of declining enrollments.

There are obvious ambiguities and even clear contradictions in the definitions used in the proposed settlement to refer to non-Black students. In computing the "base number," non-Black students include Whites, Hispanics, Asians, and Native Americans. In defining desegregated schools, the term "Minority enrollment" refers to standard definitions such as the ones used by the Department of Health, Education, and Welfare (HEW) and Chapter 220 (Laws of 1975) of Wisconsin Statutes.

This use of definitions supposedly is in line with the language contained in this Court's order of March 17, 1977, which allowed the district the flexibility and prerogative of designating Hispanic students, Native Americans, and other minority students as separate minority populations and accord them priority over other non-Black students in assignments to schools with programs designed to meet their special educational needs. However, the fact that such principle was permissive and not mandated by the court, and that there is evidence of its actual misuse by the district, suggests that the definitions may be used selectively and arbitrarily to designate some Hispanic students as "minority" and other Hispanics as "White" during desegregation student assignments. A case in point was the arbitrary assignment during the summer of 1977 of Hispanic students as "Whites" to Phillips, 20th Street, and Roosevelt schools, none of which had a bilingual program. There is also the danger that under financial pressure, MPS could

74

arbitrarily declare some students as minority for purpose of Chapter 220 reimbursement and not allow their assignment to schools that fall within, for example, the proposed racial parameters of 25% to 60% Black enrollment. We are concerned that the interests of students may not always be paramount in the plans formulated by the district, and that expediency may dictate policies and practices.

While we do not object to the proposed exemption of four predominantly Hispanic schools, we do object to the absence of measures aimed at preventing these schools from becoming minority segregated schools within the next few years. If the exemptions appear to be in line with earlier proposals made by Hispanic parents, the record will show that we have never advocated segregated schools of any kind and only insisted that exemptions be made to the movement of Hispanic students from these schools because they appeared to be serving them through sound bilingual programs available there. Nor did we ask for Hispanics to be excluded from the student count. We are mindful of mobility and other socioeconomic phenomena that affect our Hispanic communities and insist that the district must do likewise in order to ensure sound projections for proper educational planning in the future.

Another area of concern is bilingual staffing. For the past ten years MPS has operated bilingual education programs and, since 1974, the district has followed the policy guidelines adopted by the Board of School Directors regarding the type of program (maintenance) which is most beneficial and also most in tune with the desires of Hispanic parents for their children's education. It is clear from the cumulative body of law emanating from bilingual litigation and state and federal statutes that bilingual education services must be provided by teachers who are linguistically/culturally familiar with the students. The state of Wisconsin now requires that bilingual teachers be in fact bilingual in both English and the native language of the student as a criterion for reimbursement for the cost of bilingual services provided by school districts. The lack of specific language recognizing the interdependence required to facilitate bilingual student assignments and bilingual teacher assignments could hinder, if not totally impede, the implementation of legally-required bilingual programs. The Court cannot undermine the aforementioned even in the absence of a faculty desegregation component to the settlement. Language must be present to ensure that bilingual teachers who will teach in bilingual programs would be assigned and/or retained in schools in response to bilingual needs. Other supportive bilingual staff is also necessary to ensure viable bilingual programs. Thus, other bilingual/Hispanic personnel should also be assigned in accord with bilingual needs.

Finally, the Court, the defendants, and plaintiffs are all clearly mindful of the need to acquire federal aid for desegregation purposes, namely ESAA grants. However, a recent on-site review by HEW's Office for Civil Rights (OCR) brought forth charges that Milwaukee Public Schools are in violation of Title VI of the 1964 Civil Rights Act requirements relative to the provision of adequate educational services to national origin language minority students. OCR's December, 1978, letter of findings called for the designing of a plan to correct violations found and advised the district that failure to comply could endanger its ESAA grants as well as other federal funding.

OCR specifically charged that:

1. "The District (MPS) has failed to adequately identify and assess non- and limited-English speaking national origin minority students."

2. "The District has failed to take adequate affirmative steps to insure that non- and limited-English speaking children receive equally effective educational services."

3. "The District has failed to adequately identify, assess, and provide services to non- and limited-English speaking national origin minority group children in need of exceptional education instruction."

4. "The District does not provide all parents of non- and limited-English speaking national origin minority students with regular school notices in their primary language."

OCR's handling of Title VI (*Lau*) compliance in other major cities has indeed occasioned delays and even cut-offs of federal monies when districts failed to comply. It is our contention that the proposed settlement in this case must include language that would facilitate compliance efforts with OCR's requirements.

We thank the Court for its willingness to hear our concerns and those of others in this matter and hope that it will be mindful of the fact that while Hispanics were not a party to this case, we are bound to be affected by its outcome. An out-of-court settlement does allow litigants and the Court the opportunity to build in measures that would guarantee the observation and respect for the rights of our Hispanic students. Thank you.

> Tony Báez, for the CWBBAC and
> other concerned Hispanic citizens.

Notes

[1]*Armstrong* v. *O'Connell*, C.A. No. 65-C-173, Eastern District of Wisconsin (January 19, 1976). Also cited as *Amos* v. *Board of School Directors of the City of Milwaukee*, 408 F. Supp. 765 (E.D. Wisc., 1976).

[2]For an analysis of the early history of Milwaukee see: Gerd Korman, *Industrialization, Immigrants and Americanization* (Madison: The State Historical Society of Wisconsin, 1967) covering the period 1866-1921; and Bayrd Still, *Milwaukee: The History of a City* (Madison: The State Historical Society of Wisconsin, 1965) originally written in 1940.

[3]In 1920 in the United States, there were 1,043 "foreign" language newspapers, including a large number in German and Polish, many of which were published in Milwaukee. For a general discussion, see Richard Krickus, *Pursuing the American Dream: White Ethnics and the New Populism* (Garden City, N.Y.: Anchor Books, 1976), p. 141.

[4]Ibid.

[5]Andrew Greely, *Ethnicity in the United States* (New York: John Wiley and Sons, 1974), p. 17.

[6]John Buenker, "The Immigrant Heritage," in Nicholas C. Burckel, ed., *Racine: Growth and Change in a Wisconsin County* (Racine: Racine County Board of Supervisors, 1977), pp. 69-136.

[7]*Armstrong* v. *O'Connell* (Decision and Order), pp. 26-29; 35-40.

[8]Henry W. Maier, *Challenge to the Cities: An Approach to a Theory of Urban Leadership* (New York: Random House, 1966), p. 23. Maier has been mayor of Milwaukee since 1960.

[9]For an analysis of why the commission failed, see Henry J. Schmandt and William H. Standing, *The Milwaukee Metropolitan Study Commission* (Bloomington: Indiana University Press, 1965).

[10]Henry J. Schmandt, John C. Goldbach, and Donald B. Vogel, *Milwaukee: A Contemporary Urban Profile* (New York: Praeger Publishers, 1971), p. 112.

[11]David J. Kirby, T. Robert Harris, Robert L. Crain, and Christine H. Rossell, *Political Strategies in Northern School Desegregation* (Lexington, Mass.: Lexington Books, D.C. Heath and Company, 1973), pp. 20-31.

[12]Ibid., p. 35.

[13]Robert Crain, Morton Ingen, Gerald McWorter, and James Venecks, *The Politics of School Desegregation* (Chicago: Aldine Publishing Company, 1968).

[14]H. James, "Milwaukee Argues Racial Problems," *Christian Science Monitor*, October 26, 1965, p. 10 (as quoted in Schmandt et al., *Milwaukee: A Contemporary Urban Profile*, p. 151).

[15]At the time the suit was filed, the small numbers of Hispanics in the city and their lack of organized political involvement did not provide for collaboration between Hispanics and Blacks on the desegregation/schooling issues.

[16]See *A Plan to Reduce Prejudice and Discrimination in the Greater Milwaukee Area* (New York: Greenleigh Associates, Inc., 1967).

[17]Schmandt et al., *Milwaukee: A Contemporary Urban Profile*, p. 164. The Milwaukee Common Council eventually applied for Model Cities funds and received an allocation in 1969.

[18]*Racial Isolation in the Schools* (Washington, D.C.: U.S. Commission on Civil Rights, 1967).

[19]Schmandt et al., *Milwaukee: A Contemporary Urban Profile*, p. 153.

[20]For a critique of the mayor's handling of racial issues, see Peter K. Eisinger, *Patterns of Interracial Politics: Conflicts and Cooperation in the City* (New York: Academic Press, 1976).

[21]Schmandt et al., *Milwaukee: A Contemporary Urban Profile*, p. 98.

[22]Between 1974-1977 there were three Black board members, one having been appointed to fill a vacancy. She lost her bid for reelection in the spring of 1977. There has never been a Hispanic on the Milwaukee School Board. The Hispanic community demanded that one be appointed to a vacated seat in 1975, but the proposed candidate was not selected.

[23]Kirby et al., *Political Strategies in Northern School Desegregation*, p. 39.

[24]The Milwaukee Public Schools Bilingual Program grew from one bilingual classroom in 1969 at Vieau Elementary, to nineteen schools providing bilingual services in 1977 to 2,560 students, of which close to 90% were Hispanic, with a staff of seventy-four bilingual teachers, forty-five bilingual aides, thirty-one bilingual paraprofessionals, six bilingual administrators, and four bilingual counselors. In addition, the district has hired supportive-staff social workers such as bilingual and bicultural (Hispanic) special education personnel.

[25]See Board of School Directors, Milwaukee, Wisconsin, *May 7, 1974, Proceedings*, item #2, pp. 855-863.

[26]*Lau* v. *Nichols*, 414 U.S. 563 (1974).

[27]*Cisneros* v. *Corpus Christi*, 324 F. Supp. 599 (S.D. Tex., 1970).

[28]*U.S.* v. *Texas* (San Felipe-Del Rio), 342 F. Supp. 24 (E.D. Tex., 1971), aff'd per curiam, 466 F.2d. 518 (1972).

[29]*Serna* v. *Portales*, 499 F.2d 1147 (1974).

[30]*Aspira of N.Y., Inc.*, v. *Board of Education*, 394 F. Supp. 1161 (S.D., N.Y., 1975). The consent decree was actually issued on August 29, 1974.

[31]*Keyes* v. *School District No. 1* (Denver), 413 U.S. 189 (1973).

[32]*Keyes*, 521 F.2d 465 (10th Cir., 1975)

[33]See Hannah N. Geffert et al., *The Current Status of U.S. Bilingual Education Legislation*, (Papers in Applied Linguistics, Bilingual Education Series, no. 4, Applied Linguistics, 1975).

[34]In the summer of 1975 the Office for Civil Rights (OCR) released a document titled "Task-Force Findings Specifying Remedies Available for Eliminating Past Educational Practices Ruled Unlawful under *Lau* v. *Nichols.*" Later known as the "*Lau* Remedies," this document is used by OCR officials to determine whether a school district is in compliance with *Lau* requirements. Using the remedies as guidelines for

the development of a *Lau* compliance plan, the CWBBAC forced the district into surveying all Milwaukee school students to determine how many had language needs and required a program under *Lau*.

[35]Conta's "East Shore District Plan" included financial incentives for cooperative efforts and stressed the responsibility of the state in aiding school desegregation. It was not well received by the residents of the two suburbs involved nor the conservative majority of the board.

[36]Although the Supreme Court in *Milliken* v. *Bradley* 418 U.S. 717, 755 (1974) ruled out a metropolitan solution on the basis of lack of evidence of sufficient illegal actions on the part of officials, it did not rule out future use of metropolitan remedies should the evidence in a particular case support this form of remedy. As Justice Stewart said, "a cross district remedy" would have been justified if it had been shown that the state officials had "contributed to the separation of the races . . . by purposefully racially discriminatory use of state housing or zoning laws." A finding of state involvement in Delaware led a lower court in 1976 to combine Wilmington and suburban districts into one district, creating an entirely new district and school board (*Evans* v. *Buchanan*, 393 F. Supp. 428, D. Del., 1975, May 19, 1976). Also, see page 98 of the following report for clarification of the implication of the case: *Statement on Metropolitan School Desegregation* (Washington, D.C.: U.S. Commission on Civil Rights, 1977).

[37]See Milwaukee Public Schools, *INFO #1*, March 1976. About nineteen *INFO* packages have been prepared by Milwaukee schools since March 1976 and distributed to parents. Most of them have explained programs available and the desegregation process. Two of them, #4, and #9, were translated into Spanish.

[38]Programs at the "bilingual centers" varied. Some went from kindergarten to third grade, others from kindergarten to fifth grade, middle schools would go from seventh to ninth, and high schools from grades ten to twelve.

[39]This committee was comprised only of School Board members.

[40]For the text of the recommendations and other information see *Board of School Directors, Milwaukee, Wisconsin, February, March, 1976, Proceedings*, under items related to Community and Advisory Group Relations Committee.

[41]Among such groups were the Milwaukee League of Women Voters, the Sherman Park Community Association, the Urban League, and the City-Wide Bilingual Bicultural Advisory Committee.

[42]Apparently, the withdrawal by the NAACP's local branch from the legal proceedings came as a result of differences over strategies between Attorney Lloyd Barbee and the NAACP membership. The conflict culminated in a split that caused the departure of the NAACP's attorneys and the termination of the group's direct support of the case.

[43]*Armstrong* v. *O'Connell* (Decision and Order), pp. 1-2.

[44]League of Women Voters of Greater Milwaukee, *The League Bulletin*, no. 3 (March 1976).

[45]*Armstrong* v. *O'Connell*, p. 112.

[46]Ibid., p. 123.

[47]Ibid., p. 128.

⁴⁸It must be said that even though the CWBBAC came forth in support of desegregation, throughout the total desegregation planning process, top White administrators including the superintendent, and at least one Black board member, would continue to interpret the group's stand as being antidesegregation. The tendency was to generalize and claim that all Hispanics were against desegregation, thereby affecting the credibility of Hispanic groups with non-Hispanics.

⁴⁹The *Statement of Assurances* was a document prepared at this time to protect Hispanic concerns during the planning process. It is discussed later in the text and included in the Appendix.

⁵⁰For example, this happened in Houston. See *Tasby* v. *Estes,* 412 F. Supp. 1192, 1207 (N.D. Tex., 1976), following remand 517 F.2d 92 (5th Cir., 1975), cert. denied 423 U.S. 939 (1975).

⁵¹See August 1976 workcopy memo to the administration entitled *Major Issues, Assurances, and Legal Principles Affecting the Hispanic Pupil during Desegregation Efforts.* This memo was actually the first nonnegotiated draft of the *Statement of Assurances.* See Appendix A for full text.

⁵²*U.S.* v. *Texas Education Agency,* 467 F.2d 848, 869 (5th Cir., 1972): "No remedy for the dual system can be acceptable if it operates to deprive members of a third ethnic group of the benefit of equal educational opportunity."

⁵³*Keyes* v. *School District No. 1,* 521 F.2d 482, (10th Cir., 1975): "a meaningful desegregation plan" must help "Hispano school children to reach the proficiency in English necessary to learn other basic subjects." And, 413 U.S. 189, 198 (1973) where the court in *Keyes* established that the degree of segregation in any given school will depend on the ratio of Whites to the combined number of identifiable minority (Black and Hispanic) students in that school.

⁵⁴*Milwaukee Journal,* October 6, 1976, p. 12.

⁵⁵For the complete text of the *Statement of Assurances,* see Appendix A.

⁵⁶In September, 1976, a Hispanic bilingual social studies teacher was denied a transfer to South Division High School. In his place a Black, monolingual social studies teacher was appointed to fill a vacancy in the bilingual program. Among the reasons given for this action was that the Hispanic teacher was White under the court order and therefore his transfer would not enhance racial balance at the school. As a White, the teacher also had less seniority than other White teachers as well as Black teachers who, according to the terms of the contract between MPS and the Milwaukee Teachers Education Association, had first crack at the job since there were (as far as the contract's language was concerned) no bilingual social studies teachers, only social studies teachers who happened to be bilingual. The CWBBAC strongly protested this action, which on its face seemed absurd; the administration rescinded the transfer and allowed the Hispanic bilingual social studies teacher to transfer to South Division.

⁵⁷Memo from Raymond E. Williams, Acting Executive Director, Department of School Administrative Services, October 28, 1976.

⁵⁸*Report of the Special Master,* November 15, 1976, p. 6.

⁵⁹The complete title of the document is *Comprehensive Plan for Increasing Educational Opportunities and Improving Racial Balance in the Milwaukee Public Schools,* 1976.

[60]*Austin Independent School District* v. *U.S.*, 97 S. Ct. 517 (1976).

[61]"Schools Appeal to High Court," *Milwaukee Journal*, December 15, 1976, p. 1.

[62]The complete title of the document is *Memorandum in Response to Court Order Requiring Defendants to Devise and Submit a Plan for Desegregating the Milwaukee Public School System by September 30, 1978*, January 3, 1977.

[63]"McMurrin Finishes Phase 2 Blueprint," *Milwaukee Journal*, December 18, 1976, p. 1.

[64]The Wisconsin Bilingual Bicultural Act mandates bilingual education for grades K-8. It also provides seventy percent of the cost for educating limited-English-speaking-ability students. Hence, the CWBBAC was probably correct in asserting that the real motive behind the expansion was the monies coming from the state. The administration had been cooperative in the past, but CWBBAC demands for 1977-1978 probably would not have been met if the Bilingual Act had not ensured monies for reimbursement of cost.

[65]*Cisneros* v. *Corpus Christi* is an example of this application.

[66]The complete title of the document is *Reply Memorandum of Points and Authorities in Support of Motion for Intervention.*

[67]This very possibly was the first time that Black plaintiffs opposed the intervention of Hispanics in a desegregation case.

[68]*Reply Memorandum*, p. 2.

[69]*Report of the Special Master*, February 17, 1977.

[70]Ibid., p. 16.

[71]The document *Critique of the Desegregation Plans before the Special Master* was submitted to Master Gronouski on February 14, 1977 by the CWBBAC. He argued he did not have the authority to so recommend to the court.

[72]In the winter of 1977, the State Department of Public Instruction approved regulations and criteria for the certification of bilingual teachers and indeed "grandfather-claused" all bilingual teachers on the job prior to July, 1978.

[73]*Armstrong* v. *O'Connell*, Response to Comments of Parties on Remedial Recommendations of Special Master's Report of 2-17-77, March 7, 1977.

[74]Ibid., p. 7.

[75]*Armstrong* v. *O'Connell*, Order, March 17, 1977.

[76]See *Morgan* v. *Kerrigan*, Student Desegregation Plan, C.A. No. 72-911-G (May 10, 1975); (509 F.2d 580 (1st Cir.,) 1975), cert. denied 421 U.S. 963 (1975).

[77]See *Armstrong* v. *O'Connell*, Denial and Order on Motion to Intervene, April 13, 1977.

[78]Ibid., pp. 3-4.

[79]Ibid., p. 4.

[80]Ibid., p. 5.

[81]Ibid., p. 5.

[82]Ibid., p. 6.

[83]Memo to principals from Robert Tesch, Director, Division of Relationships, June 6, 1977.

[84]*Dayton Board of Education* v. *Brinkman*, 97 S. Ct. 2766 (1977).

[85]*Village of Arlington Heights* v. *Metropolitan Housing Development Corporation*, 558 F.2d. 1283 (7th Cir., 1977), cert. denied, 46 U.S.L.W. 3431 (January 9, 1978).

[86]"Text of Court Order," *Milwaukee Journal*, June 29, 1977, p. 12.

[87]*Armstrong* v. *O'Connell*, remanded by 7th Cir. September 1, 1977, No. 77-1367.

[88]The teachers' strike of spring 1977 was bitter and lengthy. For seventeen days the teachers negotiated and picketed, demanding salary increases and new protective language in the contract regarding seniority rights. The board was willing to concede some of the salary demands but sought new contractual language that would allow the superintendent to assign teachers to new programs (magnet, specialty, and bilingual) according to their qualifications in the given field. The teacher union insisted that this could only be done be seniority. Finally, the Special Master intervened to ensure that the conflict would not affect desegregation implementation. Once a settlement was reached, it was evident that the teachers lost their fight about new language for the assignment of teachers.

[89]In 1976 there were approximately 1,500 students in the bilingual programs, 95 percent of which were Hispanic. By September 1977, 2,550 students were being served, 90 percent of which were Hispanic. The total Hispanic population for the district was, at the time, 4,866.

[90]See Note 33.

[91]See Note 72 on bilingual teacher certification and Note 88 on new contractual language between the Milwaukee Schools and the teachers' union.

[92]*Columbus Board of Education* v. *Panick*, 47 U.S.L.W. 4924 (June 26, 1979); *Dayton Board of Education* v. *Brinkman*, 47 U.S.L.W. 4944 (June 26, 1979); *Regents of the University of California* v. *Allan Bakke*, U.S. 57 L Ed 2d 750, 98 S. Ct.

[93]See Appendix B for a complete description of the settlement, as publicized to the community at large by Milwaukee Public Schools.

[94]See Appendix C for the full text of the CWBBAC's statement before the court regarding the proposed settlement.

[95]One attempt at describing the dynamics of this process is found in Carlos Manuel Haro, *Mexicano/Chicano Concerns and School Desegregation in Los Angeles*, Monograph No. 9, Chicano Studies Center Publications (Los Angeles: University of California, 1977).

[96]*Cisneros* v. *Corpus Christi*; see Note 27.

[97]*Keyes* v. *School District No. 1*; see Note 31.

[98]*U.S.* v. *Texas Education Agency*; see Note 52.

[99]*Desegregation and Education Concerns of the Hispanic Community*, Conference Report, June 26-28, 1977 (Washington, D.C.: National Institute of Education).